# THE DIVINE MISSIONS

THE DIVINE MISSIONS

An Introduction

Adonis Vidu

CASCADE *Books* · Eugene, Oregon

THE DIVINE MISSIONS
An Introduction

Copyright © 2021 Adonis Vidu. All rights reserved. Except for brief quotations in critical publications or reviews, no part of this book may be reproduced in any manner without prior written permission from the publisher. Write: Permissions, Wipf and Stock Publishers, 199 W. 8th Ave., Suite 3, Eugene, OR 97401.

Cascade Books
An Imprint of Wipf and Stock Publishers
199 W. 8th Ave., Suite 3
Eugene, OR 97401

www.wipfandstock.com

PAPERBACK ISBN: 978-1-7252-8166-0
HARDCOVER ISBN: 978-1-7252-8165-3
EBOOK ISBN: 978-1-7252-8167-7

Cataloguing-in-Publication data:

Names: Vidu, Adonis, author.

Title: The divine missions : an introduction / Adonis Vidu.

Description: Eugene, OR : Cascade Books, 2021 | Includes bibliographical references.

Identifiers: ISBN 978-1-7252-8166-0 (paperback) | ISBN 978-1-7252-8165-3 (hardcover) | ISBN 978-1-7252-8167-7 (ebook)

Subjects: LCSH: Rahner, Karl, 1904–1984. | Catholic Church—Doctrines. | Theology, Doctrinal. | Trinity.

Classification: BT111.3 .V535 2021 (paperback) | BT111.3 .V535 (ebook)

VERSION NUMBER 120321

Unless otherwise indicated, Scripture quotations are from the ESV® Bible (The Holy Bible, English Standard Version®), copyright © 2001 by Crossway, a publishing ministry of Good News Publishers. Used by permission. All rights reserved.

Scripture quotations marked (NIV) are taken from the Holy Bible, New International Version®, NIV®. Copyright © 1973, 1978, 1984, 2011 by Biblica, Inc.™ Used by permission of Zondervan. All rights reserved worldwide.

In memory of
Alexandru Suărăşan

CONTENTS

Acknowledgments | xi
Introduction | xiii

1 The Nature of the Missions | 1
The Challenge of Describing Missions | 1
Progressive Manifestations | 6
Augustine's Account of the Missions | 8
    Are the Son and Spirit Disclosed in the Old Testament? | 8
    What Do the Missions Reveal? | 10
    Missions and the Trinity's Indivisible Action | 13
Ontology of the Divine Missions in Saint Thomas Aquinas | 15
    Who Sends Whom and What Does This Entail? | 15
    A New Definition: Processions and Created Effects | 16
    Resisting Mythology | 17
    The Elevation of the Creature to a Divine Mode of Existence | 18
Karl Rahner: Missions as Self-Communications | 21
Conclusion | 26

2 The Visible Missions of the Son and the Spirit | 27
Hypostatic Union | 28
    The Nature of the Union | 28
    A Mixed Relation | 29
    Receiving the Existence of the Son | 31
Theandric Life | 33
    Does the Spirit Come First? Spirit Christology | 33
    Christ's Two Operations: Divine and Human | 36
    Gradual Deification of Christ's Humanity | 37
    Does the Cross Break the Trinity? | 40

    Does the Cross Move God? | 41
    Ascension and Pentecost | 43
        Why Must the Son First Ascend? | 44
        The Spirit Comes From and Mediates Christ's Humanity | 45
    Conclusion | 48

3 The Invisible Missions | 49
    The Reality of the Invisible Missions | 50
    The Formality of the Invisible Missions | 54
        The Persons Are Assimilated into the Believer | 54
        Sanctifying Grace | 55
        Rahner's Quasi-Formality Again | 56
        Knowledge and Love as the Form of the Invisible Missions | 58
        Eleonore Stump: Mutual Within-ness | 60
        Christ's Own Love | 62
    The Finality of the Invisible Missions | 63
        Triune Personhood | 63
        A Tasting of the Persons' Personal Properties | 64
        Divine Persons as Exemplars | 66
    Missio Dei and the Order of the Missions | 67
        Developments in Missiology | 67
        Roman Catholic Theology of Religions | 69
        Evangelical Contribution: Amos Yong | 69
        Rahner: Spirit as Entelechy | 70
        Crowe: Love before Knowledge | 71
        Yong: A Pneumatology of Other Religions | 72
        The Logical Priority of the Son's Mission | 73
        The Spirit's Work in Other Religions | 75
        The Exclusivity of Christ | 77
    Conclusion | 79

4 The End of the Missions: The Vision of God | 80
    On the Possibility of the Vision | 81
        Orthodox Position | 82
        The Thomistic Position | 86
    The Vision as the Terminus of the Missions | 88
        What Is the Beatific Vision? | 89
        Our Natural Epistemic Limitations | 89
        The Light of Glory | 90

Understanding God through His Own Essence | 91
　　　Is Rahner Right after All? | 93
　　　Life of Grace and Life of Glory | 96
　　　Contemplating the Essence or the Persons? | 99
　　The Place of Christ in the Beatific Vision | 100
　　　Cabasilas on Developing a Taste for Eternity | 101
　　　Aquinas on the Vision of Christ | 102
　　　John Owen on the Vision of Christ | 103
　　　Jonathan Edwards on the Physical Vision of Christ | 106
　　Conclusion | 108

Conclusion | 109

Glossary | 113
Bibliography | 119

ACKNOWLEDGMENTS

THE FIRST PERSON THAT MUST BE ACKNOWLEDGED FALLS IN the "he made me do it" category: Michael Thompson, formerly at Eerdmans, where we worked on a previous project on the doctrine of inseparable operations. It was he that sowed the seeds for a more introductory level book exploring this unforgivably neglected dogmatic concept.

The entirety of this book was written during the fateful year 2020, during the lockdown that kicked us academics out of our school offices and pinned us at home in front of Zoom screens. Astonishingly, I found that period to be extremely conducive to writing and research generally, a coping mechanism, I am sure. I am deeply grateful for a group of fellow academics and doctoral students who have read through the whole manuscript and made incredibly helpful suggestions and insightful critiques, adding one more Zoom meeting to their calendar: Greg Parker, Andrew Johnson, Paul Sanduleac, Kimberly Kroll, Torey Teer. The manuscript was also "test driven" by a collective of Gordon-Conwell students who agreed to spend a whole semester working through the manuscript: Tom Hansen, Adila de Souza, WenHuan Lin, Sean Fei Long, Anthony Rando, William Funderburk, Zachary Hollifield. My Byington research assistant, Steven Petersheim, helped fine-tune my prose and sharpen my ideas. Finally, my wife Adriana went through the manuscript with a very fine comb, calling me out where I got carried away, calling me back to simpler writing, and consistently encouraging me throughout the process. Needless to say, all the errors and heresies herein, dormant or activated, remain mine.

For our family, the year 2020 is also the year of the passing of my father-in-law, Alexandru Suărăşan. Sandu has tasted and seen that the Lord is good. He developed a taste and hunger for God in this life, and he was recognized as a connoisseur of divinity by many who now miss him. His love of Christ was contagious, and not a few became filled with the Spirit through his witness. He had his feet planted firmly in this world, but his eyes were fixed on the coming kingdom. This book is lovingly dedicated to him.

INTRODUCTION

CHRISTIANS CONFESS THAT AT THE INCARNATION THE SON OF God didn't just *come* into the world, but he was *sent* by his Father. Likewise, at Pentecost, the Spirit was sent into the world by the Father and the Son. These *sendings*, or *missions* as they have been more commonly called, represent a theologically significant category that is easily misunderstood. The task of the present work is to provide a constructive introduction to this very important concept in trinitarian theology.

Observations of the common usage of this category among lay Christians, and not a few professional theologians, have revealed that missions are easily confused with tasks, or operations. Thus, the mission of the Son is typically understood to be that of inaugurating the kingdom, of providing atonement for sins, of seeking the lost sheep of Israel, etc. The mission of the Spirit is also understood in largely *functional* terms, viz., of being an instrument in sanctification, of providing supernatural gifts, etc. Without a doubt, the missions of the Son and the Spirit cannot be understood apart from considering their various operations. But when these operations are allowed to dominate the semantics of *mission*, something essential is all too easily lost from view. The assumption is often made that what it means for a divine person to act in the world comports no special problem. We fail to problematize what it might mean for the triune God to *act* in the world. But theology cannot simply help itself to the category of divine operations without some important qualifications.

The first thing that needs to be mentioned is that God is not any kind of finite agent. To say that God acts in the world has historically raised many questions and prompted important qualifications. Secondly, as Three-in-One, God's operations in the world are always indivisible. That is, the persons do not each have their distinct operations, since they indivisibly share the divine nature on the basis of which they act. Even though God is three "persons," these are not three beings. The persons represent distinctions within the unity of a single being. Consequently, their operations are also the operations of a single being. There is a long and complicated story about this, and we have sought to address it elsewhere.[1] But the point is that it is always the whole Trinity that acts in the world, and yet not without personal distinction.

For these reasons, the idea that the Son and the Spirit accomplish a number of tasks always needs to be coordinated with both their divine transcendence and their indivisible unity. This is exactly what the category of mission is intended to convey! It indicates that behind the various effects that are brought about, the sundry tasks that are accomplished, there is something more.

One way of putting this is to say that the category of mission shifts the conversation from the *what* to the *who*. It is not as if the variety of effects (indicated by operations) is not important, but it cannot be separated from the agent. The doctrine of the missions signals that beyond just simple effects and operations lies a divine self-communication. This is not a simple divine presence, for the divine omnipresence can be taken for granted, or a special divine operation, for such operations have taken place from the beginning of time. What is special about a mission is that a self-communication of a divine person has taken place, involving actions and operations, to be sure, but much more than these.

One reason it is important to consider the *who* question is to prevent a certain mythological understanding of the missions. This confusion can happen if we focus on the effects but forget to consider the agency, which in this case is transcendent and trinitarian. While the effects of the operation are in our world, their source—agency—is not. In the Gospel of John, Jesus is in the temple and explains his listeners' lack of comprehension to them: "You are from below; I am from above. You are of this world; I am not of this world" (John 8:23). This pertains to the very heart of the gospel, which is God with us—*Emmanuel*. While God has always acted in the past, in the fullness of time he has given us the Son, and then the Spirit. The heart of the gospel is the return of YHWH to dwell with his people; it is the very *presence* and not just the operations of God among the people.

The category of mission articulates theologically this new presence of God. It does so by discerning a pattern of God's restored presence. YHWH

---

1. Adonis Vidu, *The Same God Who Works All Things*.

comes in the sending of the Son, and then the sending of the Spirit, both of these sendings mediating the *sending Father*. While the operations pertaining to the sendings are common to the three, the missions are distinct and proper to the individual person. That is, each mission exhibits a relational pattern, an ordered flow of the eternal triune life. The mission of the Son manifests his coming forth from the Father; the mission of the Spirit manifests his spiration by the Father and the Son. Their various operations are ultimately meant to include us into this trinitarian flow of life.

We must press on to the missions, beyond just squinting at the operations, because the agent of these operations transcends them. The present book reflects more systematically upon the nature of the missions and then shows the difference this category makes. It is meant to be a guide to a conversation many are not accustomed with, but which has significant repercussions for theology in general. We shall proceed in the following manner. The first chapter analyzes the notion of a mission theologically. We start by distinguishing between progressive manifestations of the divine presence, culminating in the missions. We then introduce the two most foundational theologians of the divine missions, Saints Augustine and Aquinas. In conversation with their work a rich definition of the missions emerges, according to which a mission extends the procession of the triune persons into the world. We end the first chapter with a clarification of the distinction between missions and operations.

Having established the definition of the missions in the first chapter, we proceed to a constructive theology of the so-called visible and invisible missions. Chapter 2 discusses the visible missions of the Son and the Spirit, focusing on the hypostatic union, Christ's theandric (divine-human) life, and finally the sending of the Spirit upon Christ's ascension. The focus of chapter 3 is the invisible missions of the Son and the Spirit, that is, the interior indwelling of the two persons but also of the Father himself. We tackle several pressure points that have emerged historically in the church's reflection on these matters. The first is the question of the *formality* of the invisible missions, which is the question of what it might mean for a divine person to be *indwelling* a believer. We discuss the historic choice to consider a *created grace* as the formality of these missions. The formal priority of created grace has been relentlessly challenged by the work of Karl Rahner, whose contribution to this conversation will preoccupy us at some length. His main charge is that the formal priority of created grace obscures the distinct enjoyment of the three persons in the invisible missions. If the form of the persons' presence is only some created grace, which is the common effect of the whole Trinity, how can we be said to be distinctly related to the indwelling persons? This leads into a discussion of the finality of the invisible missions, where we argue that created grace does after all dispose us to enjoy the persons distinctly, but this enjoyment may amount to something surprising.

Throughout the book we will allude to the expected eschatological banquet, where we will enjoy the unmediated presence of God in the so-called beatific vision. It is our argument that there is an intrinsic connection between the life of grace, where we are led by the divine missions into the life of the Trinity, and the life of glory, where our hope will be consummated in the beatific vision. The fourth and final chapter addresses this issue. It demonstrates how the invisible missions are disposing us for the enjoyment of God. Finally, it argues that pride of place in the beatific vision will be the enjoyment of the incarnate Lord, in all his splendor. Thus, the missions will be shown to continue into eternity, as our enjoyment of God continues to be in some sense accompanied by our delight in the glorified Christ.

These are the main contours of the book's argument. Additional dogmatic connections will be made as we proceed. As the reader will surely note, much additional trinitarian theology is presupposed by a book of this length. To help the reader less well versed in the intricacies and technical vocabulary of trinitarian theology, a glossary has been provided. The intention is to offer an introduction to the conceptuality of the divine missions, an argument for its importance and centrality for all theology, an overview of the historical discussions and of the important contributions to the debate, plus a constructive outline of how a number of theological loci (atonement, world religions, sanctification, ecclesiology) appear from the perspective of the missions.

I

THE NATURE OF THE MISSIONS

THE AUTHOR OF THE EPISTLE TO THE HEBREWS ANNOUNCES that, after having spoken to us through the prophets in many different ways, "in these last days he has spoken to us by his Son, whom he appointed heir of all things, through whom he also created the world. He is the radiance of the glory of God and the exact imprint of his nature, and he upholds the universe by the word of his power" (Heb 1:2–3). This Son, whom God has sent, has in turn sent his Spirit of truth, a Helper, "who proceeds from the Father [and who] will bear witness about me" (John 15:26). The two missions of the Son and of the Spirit indicate a qualitatively different relationship between God and humanity. They are the fulfillment of an expectation of a return of God to Israel and to the temple, which will partly include a new and more intimate relation to the Law (Ezek 36:26–27).

THE CHALLENGE OF DESCRIBING MISSIONS

But what are these "missions" or "sendings," as they have also been called by Christian theologians? We will be working towards a definition of mission as the manifestation of a divine person in our world through union with a created thing, or effect. The notion of mission is not immediately transparent. Our imagination all too easily rushes to the concepts we have at hand. To send one on a mission, we might think, implies a motion, a change, whereby the one who is sent departs from a place and arrives at another. Careless application of this model invites a "mythological" conception of a divine mission. One mythologizes the divine missions when the one who is sent is simply regarded as an "object" in the world, without remainder. Greek mythology represents the gods in such crude spatial ways, perched as they are up on Mount Olympus and gazing down on their subjects, among which subjects they descend on occasion.

Such ways of thinking about the missions must be resisted on account of a pair of divine attributes which the church has consistently confessed. These attributes are essential to a proper understanding of the divine missions. On the one hand, God's transcendence refers to the infinite qualitative difference (as Kierkegaard calls it)[1] between God and creation. Because God is the Creator and Sustainer of every existing thing, he is not yet another item in the universe. Aquinas calls God *ipsum esse subsistens*, or subsisting being itself, as opposed to another being among beings. Moreover, since the being of God is identical to his existence, i.e., God is not a contingent being, the divine transcendence is not a property God can simply relinquish, even freely or temporarily. As the author to the Hebrews declares, the Son is the one through whom God has created the world and who upholds the universe by his powerful word. Were we to think that the Son has abandoned his transcendence during his mission, it would mean, absurdly, that he no longer sustains the world into being, or that now God sustains it in being, but without his Word. Had the incarnate Son abdicated his transcendence, worshiping him would be idolatrous, since he would be a creature. For this reason, the church has consistently, though not entirely unanimously, confessed that the one who comes into the world does not take leave of the divine essence or transcendence. He does not abdicate his throne. In the language of the trinitarian processions, the Son does not stop being begotten of the Father, from whom he is from all eternity uttered. Neither does the Spirit stop proceeding from the Father (and, or through, the Son).

A second divine attribute that must be brought to bear on the understanding of the divine missions is entailed by the divine transcendence: divine omnipresence. Since God is the transcendent Creator and Sustainer of the world, he is already present to it in virtue of his immensity. He is present to creatures as their first cause, as the one fixed point from which all are suspended. John recognizes the fact that the Word has come into the world not from without, for he was already present: "He was in the world, and the world was made through him, yet the world did not know

---

1. Kierkegaard, *Training in Christianity*, 139.

him" (John 1:10). God, we might say, is intimately present to his creatures, more intimately indeed than they are present to themselves. Everything is fully transparent to God. He repletely fills everything, by his efficiency. And yet the world did not recognize him, writes John. A forgetfulness of God reigns in the world. Despite his permeating everything, God is not recognized, and humans have turned to the worship of creatures, as opposed to God, as Paul puts it in Romans 1:22–23, "Claiming to be wise, they became fools, and exchanged the glory of the immortal God for images resembling mortal man and birds and animals and creeping things." Since God is not another being among beings, there is something understandable about this forgetfulness. While the fool says in his heart that there is no God, his foolishness does not consist in sheer ignorance. It is, rather, a matter of lack of discernment, of insight. The pattern of God's presence and activity is no longer obvious to him. The fool's heart is entangled in the cares of this world, chasing after many particular things. The fool's focus has lost its point in the immovable and transcendent God, as it became bedazzled by the diversity of particular things. The exchange of the glory of God for the images of creature indicates a disorientation of desire and of the will, a certain existential tiredness, a lack of appetite for the effort required to see through the many contingent and finite beings, to the infinite ground of them all. Instead of seeking God and submitting everything to him, creatures have turned towards themselves and each other as ultimate objects of worship. Because of our disordered condition, the omnipresence of God does not and should not make our awareness of him any easier. Neither, therefore, is it falsified by our metaphysical and existential myopia.

How is it possible to think through the idea that the Son and the Spirit have been sent, whilst honoring the principles described above, viz., that they neither left the divine transcendence nor did they arrive at a place previously devoid of their presence? The doctrine of the divine missions has emerged from a prolonged effort to discipline our ways of speaking about this mystery in ways that avoid mythologizing the missions.

We are alerted to some of the difficulties of speaking about the divine missions by Edwin Abbott's 1884 *Flatland*, an imaginative allegory of two-dimensional beings encountering beings from superior dimensions. Abbott imagines the inhabitants of a two-dimensional world, Flatland, as having geometrical shapes: some are triangles, others are squares, etc. One quickly recognizes, however, that these descriptions make sense for us, who gaze upon these geometrical figures from above, so to speak; they presuppose our three-dimensionality. To a Flatlander, however, the perception of a triangle is going to be entirely in different terms—a difference that Abbott represents by means of a sense of distance and the perception of angles. Imagine that you are facing a wall that is taller than you and you are unable to gauge the form of the structure. Only by walking around it are you able to approximate its shape. Or, remember what often happens when you are driving around without a map. Your sense of direction is often unreliable, as consulting a map will often surprise you about your actual location. If it is often difficult for a Flatlander to perceive two-dimensional geometric figures, how much more difficult would it be to understand three-dimensional objects!

Abbott imagines one such scenario in which a sphere passes through Flatland and interacts (by speaking) with one of the inhabitants. From the Flatlander's point of view, the coming of the sphere is perceived in terms of a size-shifting circle. While this would be an unusual situation for him, not being used to shapes changing sizes without a natural explanation, he still does not have a perception of the sphere as a sphere. The sphere has not changed in passing through the two-dimensional plane. Only the perception of the Flatlander has. He cannot actually perceive the sphere as a sphere, and the verbal explanations provided by the sphere fail to lead him to an understanding of the three-dimensional world, or Spaceland. What his experience provides is only an indication that other rules seem to apply, as he is not used to size-shifting circles which have the ability to appear out of nowhere, disappear without a trace, and which apparently possess the ability to see "inside" other Flatland objects and persons.

Abbott's imaginative rendering of multidimensional realities sheds some light on the complexity of thinking about the divine missions. The situation is in fact similar. We have a descent into our world of a being from a higher dimension; we might call it a transcendent dimension. Just as the sphere does not change in itself, but only in relation to Flatland, so in a mission the Son and the Spirit do not change. They remain transcendent, and they continue to proceed eternally from the Father. Their becoming manifest in the world presupposes an effect in the world, analogous to the sphere's producing a circle as an effect of its passing through Flatland. Our knowledge of the person sent is likewise going to be limited by our natural epistemic abilities. In knowing the persons we are not in fact having a comprehension of their transcendent essence, which remains inscrutable for us. We know the persons according to our created modes, and therefore a surplus of mystery always remains. As the sphere puts it, "Your country of Two Dimensions is not spacious enough to represent me, a being of Three, but can only exhibit a slice or section of me, which is what you call a Circle."[2] This statement provides an acute analogy for the nature of Christ: just as the circle is a true manifestation of the sphere in two dimensions, so the human nature of Christ is a true manifestation of the Son in the human medium.

We will return to the Flatland analogy occasionally, but we have drawn sufficient caution from it about the human possibility of adequately describing the divine missions. In entering Flatland, the sphere does not actually become a circle. While the Flatlander's only mode of description is that of a circle, and this is truthful to a certain extent, the sphere exceeds both the Flatland descriptions (epistemologically) and their perceptions (ontologically). The lesson for us is that, given the ontological difference between Creator and creatures, complete knowledge of God is impossible through our created capacities. Only if God reveals himself to us are we able to know him. But even this knowledge—as long as our capacities for comprehension remain created, that is, as long as we remain in the analogical Flatland—can only be partial. Spoiler alert: the Flatlander is ultimately able to understand the sphere once the Sphere removes him from Flatland and takes him into Spaceland. Similarly, Christians anticipate a consummation of the knowledge of God in the beatific vision, where our knowledge of God will become a true comprehension, because it will be predicated on a true union with him.

We can speak, then, about a progressive manifestation of God to the world, following the fall, whereby God speaks in various ways, through the prophets, through theophanies, and ultimately through the Son and the Spirit. The missions of the Son and the Spirit are first visible—incarnation and Pentecost (tongues of fire)—but then invisible, whereby the two persons are sent inwardly for our sanctification. This, in turn, is but a foretaste of the true union in heaven. Thirteenth-century Flemish mystic John Ruusbroec evocatively describes this process: "God is a flowing and ebbing sea which ceaselessly flows out into all his beloved according to their needs and merits and which flows back with all those upon whom he has bestowed his gifts in heaven and on earth."[3]

---

2. Abbott, *Flatland*, 58.
3. Ruusbroec, *Spiritual Espousals and Other Works*, 103.

If it is true that we can speak of a progression in our understanding of God and in his manifestation in the world, leading up to the missions, we can describe the added value of each stage as a deepening of the Christian's union with the Trinity. Raniero Cantalamessa, preacher to the papal household during John Paul II, himself commenting on Ruusbroec, puts it so well: "The Trinity sends out its word and its grace like a beneficial wave that envelops people and invites them to follow into its immensity."[4]

God looks upon a disoriented humanity, whose vision of God has become clouded because of sin, and longs to "gather [its] children together as a hen gathers her brood under her wings" (Matt 23:37). To use a familiar image from Irenaeus, the Son and the Spirit are the two hands of God at work in creation, now gathering humanity back to God, showing her what was there all along (Rom 1:19–20), if only it had the eyes to see and ears to hear.

PROGRESSIVE MANIFESTATIONS

Now that we have seen that the transcendent God reaches out and draws the world back to himself, it is time to distinguish between the various modes of God's self-manifestation in redemptive history. The missions of the Son and the Spirit are the culmination of a process whereby God draws the creature nearer to him. In *Flatland*, the sphere gradually makes itself manifest, first by speech, then by appearing and disappearing, then by making objects appear and disappear, finally by demonstrating privileged knowledge of the square. Prior to the divine missions, there is a gradual manifestation of God to his people. It will be helpful initially to lay out the various categories, as these have been consolidated through the centuries of theological reflection.

1. *Theophanies*. Theophanies can be described as visible manifestations of God, either in human form (e.g., Abraham's visitors at Mamre) or non-human form (e.g., burning bush), whether in reality or in dreams/visions (Dan 7). As we shall see, the theophanies raise interesting questions in relation to the divine missions, chief among which is whether there was a manifestation of the divine persons, and in particular the person of the Son, prior to the incarnation. In theophanies, however, no apparent enduring union exists between God and these

---

4. Cantalamessa, *Contemplating the Trinity*, 53.

forms (either Abraham's visitors or the burning bush). It should also be pointed out that theophanies may involve the angel of the Lord, a celestial being representing God and often accepting worship as God.

2. The *visible mission* of the Son in the incarnation. Here we speak of a hypostatic union that has taken place once and forever between the eternal Word and a human nature. Here God makes himself visible in the human face of Jesus Christ.

3. The *visible mission* of the Spirit at Pentecost. Before Pentecost, the Spirit was visibly made manifest at Jesus's baptism and when Christ breathes on his disciples, giving them the Holy Spirit. These pre-Pentecost manifestations raise important questions about the order of the two missions. Yet they are distinguished from the outpouring of the Spirit, also visible in the form of tongues of fire, at Pentecost. In distinction from the hypostatic union, no such final conjunction exists between the Spirit and these created realities (baptismal dove, breath, tongues of fire), prompting some to call them symbolic missions.

4. The *invisible missions* of the Spirit and the Son. Following from Pentecost, where the Spirit is visibly made manifest, there ensues an inward, invisible indwelling of the Spirit, who is now "poured into our hearts" as the love of God (Rom 5:5). Whilst some have reserved the category of *indwelling* for the Holy Spirit alone, we know that the Son also has an invisible interior mission (John 14:23) and that he has promised to be with us forever (Matt 28:20). Questions remain about the form of Christ's presence with believers, given that he has ascended with his physical body, just as questions persist about the form of the Spirit's own indwelling. We are going to be addressing the majority of these in the appropriate context.

The progression in these manifestations is arguably from the theophanic to the visible missions of the Son and the Spirit and then to the invisible missions of the Son and Spirit. This is an arguable sequence because, as we shall see, some have suggested that the visible mission of the Son in the incarnation is prepared by an invisible mission of the Son to Mary. This observation notwithstanding, we shall for the moment assume the traditional sequence of theophanies—visible missions—invisible missions.

The question before us is this: how can a mission be defined in order to bring out the distinction between the "long ago" and "in these last days" of Hebrews 1? What is so special about this final revelation through the

Son? In what consists its "added value" in relation to the manifestations of the divine in the Old Testament? The first systematic treatment of this issue is to be found in Saint Augustine of Hippo, whose *De Trinitate* (*On the Trinity*) is a painstaking engagement with the two missions.

AUGUSTINE'S ACCOUNT OF THE MISSIONS

Are the Son and Spirit Disclosed in the Old Testament?

Augustine defines a mission as the *manifestation of a divine person*. There are two senses of being sent, he explains: showing himself to the world and being perceived by someone's mind.[5] The first sense is, so to speak, from the perspective of the one sent: someone is revealing himself to the world. The second sense is from the perspective of the recipient of the manifestation: someone perceives the one who is sent. Books 2 and 3 of *De Trinitate* assess whether the divine persons were manifested in the Old Testament. Throughout the discussion, Augustine insists that what takes place in the OT *cannot* be understood as a disclosure of the persons. The reason for this is that the Son has no human nature before the incarnation. The *economic theologians*[6] had supposed that the Son is the intrinsically visible member of the Trinity and that these theophanies are, to use Edmund Hill's term, "pre-performance appearances" of the Son. However, Augustine understood that, strictly speaking, there are no personal missions prior to the incarnation. To suppose otherwise, as Hill explains, would have "blurred the distinction between his [the Son's] humanity and his divinity, blurred the complete truth of his divinity, and blurred the difference between the Old and the New Testaments, that is, between the old and new dispensations and economies."[7]

Shouldn't one understand at least some of the theophanies as the manifestation of some triune persons? He concludes that Christ could not have been one of the men who appeared to Abraham at Mamre.[8] The three

---

5. Augustine, *Trinity*, 4.28.

6. These are theologians from the earliest phases of trinitarian reflection, who understood the distinctions between the divine persons only in terms of the economy and failed to see how they reflect eternal and immanent distinctions. So, for example, the Son is that mode by which God is visible to creation, and who can be discerned going all the way back to Genesis.

7. E. Hill, *Mystery of the Trinity*, 85.

8. Augustine, *Trinity*, 2.19–20.

angels represent and manifest but are not the divine persons. At Mamre, in particular, we have an "episode" that is a "visible intimation by means of visible creations of the equality of the triad, and of the single identity of substance in the three persons."[9] The burning bush episode is similarly inconclusive with regards to the manifestation of a particular person, as Augustine surmises that it is unclear which divine person the angel is playing the part of. With regards to Mount Sinai, it is also undecidable which person, if any, is manifested, although Augustine tentatively entertains an *appropriation* to the Holy Spirit.[10]

Theophanies take place by way of "creature control," in Augustine's formulation.[11] That is, God deploys created means, whether supernatural creatures such as angels or natural creatures such as clouds, bushes, etc., as instruments for the manifestation of the divine being. Yet there is no *intrinsic connection* between the creature and the divine persons. At most Augustine is prepared to concede a symbolic value to the various creaturely mediums, such as the representation of plurality and unity at Mamre.

One underlying interest in book 2 of *De trinitate* is to reject the notion, propounded by some of Augustine's opponents, that the Son is the intrinsically visible member of the Trinity, unlike the Father, who is characterized by invisibility. The sending of the Son was being deployed by heretics to argue for a subordination of the Son to the Father. Against the argument that the Father alone is intrinsically invisible, and thus in some sense superior, Augustine appeals to the vision of the Ancient of Days and of the son of man in Daniel 7. He concedes that "both the Father bestowing the Kingdom and the Son receiving it appeared to Daniel in physical form."[12] Here again, despite the fact that the persons are indicated, God is not manifested as he is in himself, "but in symbolic manner as times and circumstances required."[13] The divine substance remains invisible, and yet God presents himself to the external gaze of men, whether awake or asleep (Dan 7). The conclusion of book 2 is helpful: "that nature, or substance, or essence, or

---

9. Augustine, *Trinity*, 2.20.

10. This is on the basis of the parallelism between the fifty days that elapsed between Passover and the giving of the law at Sinai, and between the crucifixion and Pentecost (Augustine, *Trinity*, 2.26). To say that some operation is *appropriated* to a trinitarian person means that, despite the persons' indivisible operation, one such act is particularly revealing of and appropriate to one of the persons.

11. Augustine, *Trinity*, 2.25.

12. Augustine, *Trinity*, 2.33.

13. Augustine, *Trinity*, 2.32.

whatever else you may call that which God is, whatever it may be, cannot be physically seen; but on the other hand we must believe that by creature control the Father, as well as the Son and the Holy Spirit, could offer the senses of mortal men a token representation of himself in bodily guise or likeness."[14] Even though God remains invisible in himself, he makes us alert to his presence and activity by causing changes in our world.

Creature control, in Augustine's signature theological move, is handled by the whole Trinity. That is, the conjuring up of whatever physical medium for the representation and manifestation of God, whether or not that manifestation hints at the diversity of persons (Mamre) or only at the unity of substance (Exod 3), is the common work of the Trinity. That is, the divine persons do not each efficiently cause the respective created form which stands in for them. In this sense, the theophanies are the common work of the whole Trinity, and therefore they do not explicitly and intrinsically manifest the persons. What we might call the *explicit and intrinsic manifestation* of the persons is reserved for the true missions of the Son and the Spirit, as we shall see.

What Do the Missions Reveal?

The fifth chapter of book 4 is getting at the heart of the missions as the revelation of the divine persons. Weighing on Augustine is the burden of rejecting the inference from the Son's being sent to his inferiority to the Father. This had been the opinion of some theologians, who had argued that being sent implies being less than the sender. Augustine's response is that only insofar as the Son was made, that is only in terms of his human nature, can he be said to be less than the Father. However, the recognition that all things were made through the Son (John 1:3) leads us to "confess that he whom we call less when he had been sent was equal to the one who sent him not only before he was sent and so made, but before all things were."[15] The fact that the whole universe was made through the Son divulges his equality to the Father.

Augustine then explains that "the reason why the Son is said to have been sent by the Father is simply that the one is the Father and the other the Son."[16] This gets us at the heart of the issue: the reason the Son is sent is

---

14. Augustine, *Trinity*, 2.35.
15. Augustine, *Trinity*, 4.26.
16. Augustine, *Trinity*, 4.26.

because he himself comes from the Father. The mission of the Son reveals his procession, that is, it reveals his eternal identity as the only begotten one of the Father. "Not because one is greater and the other less, but because one is the Father and the other the Son; one is the begetter, the other begotten; the first is the one from whom the sent one is; the other is the one who is from the sender."[17]

The conundrum here is, what do the missions indicate? Does the fact of the Son's being sent reveal anything in particular about the identity of the Son? Now, of course, we may take it that the fact that he is sent and not sender is entirely arbitrary and accidental. In this case we would have to question whether the Son is really manifested in his mission. The logic of this response is not altogether transparent, but it is solidly steeped in trinitarian grammar. The Son, according to this grammar, is nothing but the divine essence taken in terms of this relation of begetting/being begotten, which is the relation to the Father, as the personal property of the Son. Because God is a single and simple essence, the persons of the Trinity do not partition the divine essence and therefore do not possess distinct attributes from each other, except one: their "origination" from one another. The persons share the essential divine goodness, power, will, and knowledge. The only thing they do not share, and therefore their only distinguishing marks, are the oppositional terms entailed by the relations of origin: unbegotten-begotten, in the case of the Father-Son. Thus, if the mission does not indicate these relations of origin, it does not disclose anything about the personal identity of the person sent.

Now, insofar as we suppose the mission reveals something, it is either the substance or the relations within the unity of this substance. In the case of the former, being sent from the Father would indicate an inferiority of substance in relation to the Father. Were the latter true, being sent from the Father would *only* show that within the unity of the divine substance, the Son is *from* the Father. The latter is precisely Augustine's solution: the reason the Son is sent is because he is Son, begotten, from the Father.

Without hesitation, the argument is thus clinched: "In the light of this we can now perceive that the Son is not just said to have been sent because the Word became flesh, but that he was sent in order for the Word to become flesh, and by his bodily presence to do all that was written. That is, we should understand that it was not just the man who the Word became that was sent, but that the Word was sent to become man. For he was not sent

17. Augustine, *Trinity*, 4.27.

in virtue of some disparity of power or substance or anything in him that was not equal to the Father, but in virtue of the Son being from the Father, not the Father from the Son."[18] The word became flesh, which is to say he became a creature, because he was sent. It is not because he is a creature that the Word was sent. Rather, the Word became a creature because he was sent. To put it in terms of a logical distinction, the *createdness* of the Word, namely his created human nature, is consequent upon his *being sent*, while his being sent is a consequence of his relational position within the unity of the Godhead, as the Father's Son.

The qualitative difference between the Old Testament representations of the Trinity and the mission of the Son is expressed in terms of the act of union between the Word and the flesh: "Angelic beings could represent this person beforehand in order to foretell him; they could not take him over and just be him."[19] Theophanies are anticipations, foretellings, or *prolepses*[20] of the missions; on the other hand, the mission entails a real "coupling"[21] between man and the Word of God. In this sense, the Son had not been given before.

The same cannot be said, in Augustine's opinion, about the Spirit, who had been given before, since by him the prophets spoke. One must allow, in the case of the outpouring of the Spirit, for some special quality which had been absent before, but Augustine claims the license to affirm this about the Spirit, since the Spirit had not assumed union with flesh. He allows that the Spirit had been given before, since, unlike the Son's incarnation, the Spirit's mission does not entail assuming flesh. The physical breath that came out of Christ when he gave the Spirit to his disciples was a "convenient symbolic demonstration that the Holy Spirit proceeds from the Son as well as from the Father."[22] But, since it cannot be one Spirit that he breathed on the disciples (John 20) and another Spirit that was given at Pentecost, Augustine all but implies that there existed a mission of the Spirit in the Old Testament saints. This cannot be said about the Son, since he was incarnate in time.

---

18. Augustine, *Trinity*, 4.27.

19. Augustine, *Trinity*, 4.30.

20. We have encountered this terminology in Allison and Kostenberger, *Holy Spirit*, 348–49.

21. Augustine, *Trinity*, 4.30.

22. Augustine, *Trinity*, 4.29.

Missions and the Trinity's Indivisible Action

Augustine's theology of the divine missions pivots around the notion of the manifestation of the persons. Old Testament theophanies *represent* the persons, without revealing their proper identities. A representation acts like a placeholder, signaling *that* something or someone exists or acts. A manifestation, on the other hand, is a natural and non-arbitrary disclosure of *who* acts. The mission of the Son is by way of the union between the Word and the flesh. The mission of the Spirit entails a visible manifestation, but without coupling, or union. Throughout this exposition, we are aware of the limitations of the human mind to comprehend and to represent the persons. The persons are of one substance and thus "act inseparably. But they cannot be manifested inseparably by creatures which are so unlike them, especially material ones."[23] This conviction is based in the ontological difference between God and humanity. What is perfect unity at the level of the Godhead is manifested separately. Speaking about the baptism of Jesus, Augustine explains that the created effects nevertheless manifest the persons distinctly: "The Trinity together produced both the Father's voice and the Son's flesh and the Holy Spirit's dove, though each of these single things *has reference* to a single person."[24]

An economic unfolding of the perfect trinitarian unity takes place in such a way that the individual correspondents for each divine person, the signs, or that which have reference to the persons, are separated and distinct from one another. Much like the refraction of light spreads out in our experience the many colors, which are nevertheless unified in the light itself, so the Trinity is spread out across intervals of time and space in the economy. This is the equivalent of the circular footprint of the sphere as it passes through Flatland. We need not be surprised at this discrepancy, which is the natural consequence of the infinite qualitative difference.

Granting this qualitative difference, one may legitimately wonder whether anything is truly revealed about the divine persons. If Old Testament theophanies merely represent and indicate the persons, is there a truer self-communication of the Trinity in the missions? With respect to the mission of the Son, Augustine writes, "The very Word of God was made

---

23. Augustine, *Trinity*, 4.30.

24. Augustine, *Trinity*, 4.30. This is one of the places where Augustine applies the analogy of memory, understanding, and will, to show how three faculties that are inseparably deployed in the production of the words "memory," "understanding," and "will," are nevertheless individually referred to by the respective words.

flesh, that is, was made man, without however being turned or changed into that which he was made."[25] The incarnation thus entails a creation, which is the human nature of Christ, and yet Christ can be both God and man. And yet Augustine does not analyze further the question of how a physical appearance, which is a creation, and which therefore needs to be produced by way of created means, can truly communicate a divine person, given the ontological difference entailed. He simply claims that one can be another.

And then he follows up with this: "If this is difficult to understand, then you must purify your mind with faith, by abstaining more and more from sin, and by doing good, and by praying with the sighs of holy desire that God will help you to make progress in understanding and loving."[26] We may be tempted to dismiss this as a typical rhetorical flourish, completely idle in relation to the whole argument. But this would be a mistake. What he indicates here is that in order to understand how it is possible that the human flesh is also the Son of God, a higher perception is needed, a transformation of the mind and the soul, in fact an elevation of these above their natural powers. In grasping such eternal truths, he earlier explained, we are in fact in heaven, since they are beyond the natural powers of the human mind, just as it is beyond the powers of Flatlanders to understand three-dimensional objects. Such a spiritual perception, however, is precisely the Word's and the Spirit's to accomplish. The signs deployed in the manifestation of the persons, the flesh, the voice, the dove, are not ends in themselves, but meant to guide us in a process of holistic transformation, a process which naturally starts with the senses but ends at a spiritual level.

Now we may understand why theophanies could never lead to an understanding of the persons. Not only were the forms produced by the angels not *united* to the eternal persons, but such a perception can take place only through the transformation of the human soul brought about by just such a union with God.

To summarize our incursion into Augustine's theology of the missions, it may be said that his signal contribution is to have clarified what the sending of a transcendent person into a finite world might mean; how this takes place through created means; how the older theophanies, although similarly employing created effects, do not truly manifest the persons but, at best, only represent them. Finally, that the mission of the Son (in particular) entails a real union, unlike anything else in the past, and yet a union

25. Augustine, *Trinity*, 4.31.
26. Augustine, *Trinity*, 4.31.

that does not change the divine person. While Augustine begins to scratch at the idea that the missions reveal the processions, he does not explain how that happens. It will fall on the shoulders of Saint Thomas Aquinas to illuminate the manner in which the processions are extended into creation by the missions.

ONTOLOGY OF THE DIVINE MISSIONS IN SAINT THOMAS AQUINAS

Who Sends Whom and What Does This Entail?

The relationship between the missions and the processions is of fundamental theological importance because, as we have seen, one may (mistakenly) induce from the mission a certain hierarchy among the divine persons. Augustine responds by insisting that the missions are illuminating the relational distinctions within God, not a distinct substance of the persons. Other responses have been given as well. Saint Ambrose, who is roughly contemporaneous with Augustine, responds to this objection by accepting that the Son was also sent by the Spirit, appealing to Isaiah 48:15–16 and 61:1. He takes this as a demonstration of their unity: "Behold their unity, inasmuch as whom God the Father sends, the Son sends also, and whom the Father sends, the Spirit sends also."[27]

Seven centuries after Augustine, Peter Lombard, whose *Sentences* became the required theology textbook for medieval divinity studies, agrees with Ambrose that both the Father and the Spirit send the Son.[28] In the context it becomes clear that he is sent by the Father, the Spirit, and by himself. "This is the joint work of the Father and Son and Holy Spirit."[29] On the other hand, Bonaventure disagrees that the Spirit can be said to send the Son, since the one who sends possesses an authority over the one sent—which is not something he would want to grant to the Spirit.[30] Quite clearly, it remained somewhat confusing the manner in which a mission indicates a procession, given that, at least in the West, it was agreed that the Spirit proceeds from the Father and the Son, while the Son proceeds from the Father alone. But if it can be properly said that the Son is sent by the

---

27. Ambrose, *Fide* 2.9, ss. 76.
28. Lombard, *Sentences: Book 1*, dist. 15, ch. 3.
29. Lombard, *Sentences: Book 1*, dist. 15, ch. 4.3.
30. Bonaventure, *Breviloquium*, 52.

Father and the Spirit, then his sending doesn't echo his procession. These questions will receive an authoritative solution in the *Summa Theologica* (*ST*) of Thomas Aquinas.

A New Definition: Processions and Created Effects

The place of the doctrine of the missions in the *ST* follows the treatment of the divine persons and their relationship with the substance. Once our understanding of the immanent Trinity is properly ordered, we then move to the missions in question 43. The first article asks "Whether a Divine Person Can Be Properly Sent?" The very first objection invokes the inference from being sent to being lesser. If a person is properly sent, so the objection goes, it means that he is inferior to the sender. Aquinas responds by first defining a mission: "The notion of mission includes two things: the habitude [or relation, disposition] of the one sent to the sender; and that of the one sent to the end whereto he is sent."[31] These two relations are the relation of origin, or the procession;[32] and the relation to the term, or the created reality involved in a mission. He continues to explain that the mission of a divine person can be taken "as meaning in one way the procession of origin from the sender, and as meaning a new way of existing in another; thus the Son is said to be sent by the Father into the world, inasmuch as he began to exist visibly in the world by taking our nature; whereas He was previously in the world (Jo. 1.1)."[33]

This is a particularly elegant definition, and it takes us considerably further than Augustine's explanations keyed to the notion of manifestation. The mission isn't merely the manifestation of a person. That would entail that the person of the Father can also have a mission because he has also been manifested (Daniel's vision of the Ancient of Days, the voice from heaven, etc.). What Augustine's framework did not catch was the *directionality* of a mission. Missions are not simply manifestations of this or that person but precisely of a trinitarian relationality. They are, to use Dominic Legge's terminology, *vectors*.[34] This builds on the foundation of

---

31. Aquinas, *Summa Theologica* [*ST*] I, q. 43, art. 1, *responsio*.

32. "Origin" is meant here not in the sense of a "beginning," but of "source." The Son comes *from* the Father; the Spirit is *from* the Father and Son; the Father himself is *not from* anyone.

33. Aquinas, *ST* I, q. 43, art. 1, *responsio*.

34. Legge, *Trinitarian Christology of Thomas Aquinas*, 52.

the persons understood as "subsistent relations," another technical and, for many, confusing term consolidated by Aquinas. Contrary to the modern psychological understanding of persons as centers of consciousness, Aquinas understands persons as relations. If the persons each had their own consciousness, there would be three gods. So the persons share everything in the divine substance, except where there is a distinction by relative opposition.[35] The persons are, in fact, precisely this relational directionality within the unity of the divine essence, and constituting this essence as well. Aquinas's approach, on the other hand, is able to explain how the mission is, in fact, an external and temporal procession.[36]

Resisting Mythology

This does not involve the divine person in any sort of change, which is another objection Aquinas must consider, leading to another essential explanation: "That a divine person may newly exist in anyone, or be possessed by anyone in time, does not come from change of the divine person, but from change in the creature."[37] To come to exist newly in anyone presupposes the fact that God (and the person sent) is already omnipresent to the creature. A change in the mode of presence is thus not a change in God but a change in the creature. The sphere does not change by being present in Flatland. Rather, a change takes place in the receiving medium.

This correction mitigates the impulse to mythologize. It comes rather naturally to us to think, in categories we are accustomed to, about divine persons going up and down an "ontological ladder." By this we mean beings moving from one level of reality to another. But in fact there is no ontological slide between the transcendent God and contingent creation. God's transcendent essence is not something he might put aside, as if it were an accidental accoutrement. God simply is his essence, and all his essential attributes are identical to himself. For this reason, he cannot stop being himself. The mythological error is to think that God has *become* an object in the world, and by that to mean that he is no longer divine but rather a created being. Such an error has historically been, especially in the popular understanding of the faith, only an arm's length away.

---

35. Cf. Aquinas, *ST* I, q. 28, art. 3; q. 29, art. 4.
36. Aquinas, *ST* I, q. 43, art. 2, *responsio*.
37. Aquinas, *ST* I, q. 43, art. 2, ad. 2.

However, to say that a triune person was sent in the world should not be taken as changing the person, since he requires no motion by which to arrive here. But the notion of mission entails a fundamental change in the creature. Let's switch analogies and think of a magnet that, by just being itself and not doing anything different, attracts a needle that eventually becomes attached to one of the poles of the magnet. Resulting from this attachment, the needle is not only positioned differently, but it acquires something from the magnet, specifically its magnetic charge. The needle is attracted by the whole magnet to itself, but it is attached specifically to one of the poles of the magnet. This serves as an apt illustration for the mission of the Son. The human nature of Christ is like the needle, attracted and embraced by the whole Trinity, but attached specifically to the Son, from whom it acquires its mode of existence as the Son. The needle does not itself become a magnet, yet it receives the charge of one of the poles, i.e., the mode of existence of just one of the poles. In the mission of the Son, therefore, a human nature, which, as a creature, is produced by the inseparable operation of the whole Trinity, is united specifically to the Son.

The Elevation of the Creature to a Divine Mode of Existence

Herein we see the improvement over Augustine's incipient formulations. The human nature does not merely designate the Son, or represent the Son, or manifest the Son, but rather it acquires the Son's specific mode of existence, of being from the Father. The human nature is *elevated* beyond its natural capacities and operation to acquire the mode of existence of the Son specifically. Note that the human essence does not change; it does not go up the ontological ladder to become divine. Rather, it only receives one of the *modes of existence* of the Trinity, that of the Son. Thus, the human nature of Christ truly *exists* as the Son of God, without it being essentially divine.

The qualitative distinction is preserved, but the created reality doesn't merely signify, or designate, the supernatural person. Rather, it acquires the very mode of existence of this person! But Aquinas wants to exercise maximum caution here: the receiving nature must retain its integrity, even if it is possessed by a divine person. Thus, in the third article of the same question 43, Aquinas insists that the invisible mission is "only according to the gift of sanctifying grace."[38] Here Aquinas is referring specifically to the mission of the Spirit, or to the indwelling. He explains that "the Holy

---

38. Aquinas, *ST* I, q. 43, art. 3.

Ghost proceeds temporally for the creature's sanctification. . . . Since then the creature's sanctification is by sanctifying grace, it follows that the mission of the divine person is only by sanctifying grace."[39] God, the Angelic Doctor shows, is already present in all things by his essence, power, and presence. But in rational creatures, God may also be present as the object known is present in the knower, and the beloved in the lover.[40] This happens by sanctifying grace, and in no other way. Therefore the Spirit is said to be invisibly[41] sent into rational creatures by sanctifying grace.

This is another significant move, and it can be seen to follow from the earlier principle that a new manner of existence of God means that the creature changes, rather than the divine person. But what is this change, except the sanctification of the creature? The presence of a divine mission entails the elevation of the creature, beyond its natural capacities, to a supernatural participation in the divine life. This can be variously called sanctification, deification, and even adoption. Aquinas has in mind here not merely a judicial declaration but an actual and ontological transformation. In the visible mission of the Son, his incarnation, this is the conferring to Christ's human nature of the mode of sonship. Just like the needle is elevated beyond its natural capacity to become magnetized, so the human nature of Christ supernaturally receives that which belongs to the Son. Conversely, as we shall see, in the invisible missions of the Son and the Spirit, the creature receives a participation in the personal existence of the two persons. For Aquinas, since this is a participation the creature is not naturally capable of, it entails an elevation by way of a supernatural gift, which is sanctifying grace.

Against the objection that the person is not truly sent, but only his created gifts, Aquinas responds that by this sanctifying gift we are precisely enjoying the person: "We are said to possess only what we can freely use or enjoy: and to have the power of enjoying the divine person can only be according to sanctifying grace. And yet the Holy Ghost is possessed by man, and dwells within him, in the very gift itself of sanctifying grace. Hence the Holy Ghost himself is given and sent."[42] The Spirit is not really "buffered" by sanctifying grace. Rather, the latter is the formality by which the former may be received into a human nature. Aquinas also adds that this grace

---

39. Aquinas, *ST* I, q. 43, art. 3, *sed contra*.

40. Aquinas, *ST* I, q. 43, art. 3, *responsio*.

41. We will discuss the distinction between visible and invisible missions in chs. 2 and 3 below.

42. Aquinas, *ST* I, q. 43, art. 3, *responsio*.

"disposes the soul to possess the divine person."[43] We should not understand by this that there is some preparation different than the very presence of the Spirit but rather that the Spirit indwells by adapting the creature, or by disposing it to receive a supernatural presence.

We will return to the formality of the indwelling below. Let us now turn to article 8 of the same auestion 43, where Aquinas asks: "Whether a Divine Person Is Sent Only by the Person Whence He Proceeds Eternally?" As we have seen, some confusion persisted over this particular issue, even up to Lombard. In the *sed contra*, he appeals to the same text in Isaiah 48 and agrees that a divine person may be sent from one from whom he does not proceed. However, Aquinas recognizes the difference of opinion among theologians. He notes one explanation, whereby the Son is sent by the Spirit "as regards His human nature,"[44] conceding some truth to it, but then offering the following synthesis, which we may quote at length: "If the sender be designated as the principle of the person sent, in this sense not each person sends, but that person only Who is the principle of that person who is sent; and thus the Son is sent only by the Father; and the Holy Ghost by the Father and the Son. If, however, the person sending is understood as the principle of the effect implied in the mission, in that sense the whole Trinity sends the person sent."[45]

Here we see again the explanatory power of Aquinas's account of the missions as extended processions. If a mission is considered from the point of view of the procession, the person is only sent by the one from whom he originates, because the processions are *divisa*, or separable. If, on the other hand, we consider it from the point of view of the created effect, then the person may be said to be sent by the whole Trinity. With this fine distinction, Aquinas has introduced greater clarity about the relationship between the missions and the processions.

The sendings and the processions are not two different realities[46] but the same reality considered from different angles. In the missions we participate in the very life of the Trinity, guided by the terms of the missions, the created reality used by God for this end. The missions are vectors into

---

43. Aquinas, *ST* I, q. 43, art. 3, ad. 2.

44. Aquinas, *ST* I, q. 43, art. 8, *responsio*.

45. Aquinas, *ST* I, q. 43, art. 8, *responsio*. Aquinas is using the terminology of "principle" in the sense of cause, or source. Thus, the principle of a person means the origin of the person; the principle of the effect means the cause of the effect.

46. Lombard, *Sentences: Book 1*, dist. 14, ch. 1.1.

the very life of God, employing visible created means (the flesh of Christ, tongues of fire, etc.) and invisible sanctifying grace (the love poured into our hearts by the Spirit, Rom 5:5) for our sanctification and elevation to supernatural life.

KARL RAHNER: MISSIONS AS SELF-COMMUNICATIONS

The missions are not wearing their meaning on their sleeves. We have explained that the reason for this is the Creator-creature distinction and infinite qualitative difference. Doesn't this make a mockery out of revelation, however? Does this separable unfolding of an inseparable being and activity amount to a true self-communication of God? It seems as if the so-called immanent and economic Trinities are vastly different from one another. This impression is given by at least two factors in this Augustinian-Thomistic tradition of the divine missions. One factor is the rule of the inseparability of divine operations *ad extra*, which stipulates that, given the unity of the divine essence, all the operations of the triune persons in the world are indivisible. Whatever one of the Trinity does, the others do as well—and not merely in the sense of a cooperative action, where they help out or make various supplemental contributions. The rule is quite simply insisting that there is no individual action *ad extra* belonging to any single triune person.

Augustine hinted at this rule when referring to the flesh of Christ, the voice from heaven, and the dove at Jesus's baptism. The three persons are inseparable in their operation, and yet they are manifested separably for us by the various creaturely means. He knows that this rule has generated some confusion in the churches, and he addresses this in his "Sermon 52." The worry was that the rule leads to the confusion of the persons. His solution is to say that the whole Trinity produces the created effects involved in a divine mission, and yet these have reference to just one of the divine persons. In the case of the incarnation, the human flesh of Christ is produced by the common operation of the Trinity, yet it is only the Son that became flesh, and not the Father or the Spirit. Similarly for the voice from heaven and the dove.

The second factor that contributes to the apparent severing of the economic and immanent trinities in this tradition is the claim made by Aquinas that any of the divine persons might have become incarnate. If the flesh of Christ is commonly produced by the Trinity as a whole, it presumably makes no difference to this flesh that it is attached to the Son himself—and not to any of the other two persons.

In modern theology Karl Rahner poignantly raises an objection against this tradition. In Rahner's opinion, this model does not allow us to imagine relations to the divine persons taken distinctly and in their proper identity. The rule produces a uniformization of our relations to the Trinity as a whole. But if relations to the divine persons taken individually are not possible, we cannot really say that a self-communication of the divine persons has really taken place. We relate to the Trinity as a whole—even though we *appropriate* certain of these relations to one person or another. By appropriation we mean that certain of these relations, or certain divine operations, even though inseparable and common, nevertheless reveal something about this or that divine person.

Rahner argues that if we truly are to make sense of the self-communication of the divine persons, that is, if each of these persons is to be revealed to us in their *propria*, then we have to accept that there can be non-appropriated, or non-common, relations between the individual divine persons and creation. That is, we have to be able to say that there are aspects in the world, or created effects, that are not accounted for by the single divine causality but by a personal causality of the persons. But what might such a causality be?

There would be an easy way out for Rahner, which would be to simply go the way of so-called *social trinitarianism*. According to this trinitarian approach the persons are not understood so much as relations that subsist in the unity of the divine substance but separate centers of consciousness and activity, with their own intellect, understanding, the whole set of personal qualities. The unity of God in such an account is of a collective sort. The persons mutually inhere in one another, but they do not share essential attributes. Rahner is of the opinion that such a solution is ultimately destructive of Jewish-Christian monotheism and therefore cannot be adopted. Social trinitarianism admits that the persons act individually in the world, even though they mutually indwell each other. When one person acts, the others are also "carried along" for the action, but they approve and support, rather than sharing the agency for that action. The reason such a position is rightly rejected by Rahner is that it undermines the ultimate biblical basis for trinitarian monotheism, which is the biblical ascription to Jesus and to the Spirit of the very same actions that God is supposed to be operating, primarily the act of creation, but also redemption, sanctification, judgment, etc.

But if we cannot ascribe distinct actions to the divine persons, what remains? Rahner's suggestion is intriguing but is also one of the most obscure proposals in modern theology. Rahner is testing whether any type of causality can be ascribed to the persons taken distinctly. Causality is that relation by which one thing or event can be said to originate in another. Aristotle had established that there are four kinds of causality. In *efficient* causality, a principle brings about the existence of an effect, or a change in a term. Michelangelo is the efficient cause of the statue *David*, presently in the Uffizi in Florence. The sculptor efficiently acts on the block of marble to shape it into this statue. In *material* causality, a thing is provided its material substrate, which is formed into this or that thing. Aristotle had argued that every existing thing is a compound of matter and form. In reality there exists no such thing as unformed matter, so this is a conceptual distinction. The material cause of Michelangelo's *David* is the material out of which it is formed. We could say the marble, but we would be mistaken, since marble is already a formed "matter." A third kind of cause is the *final* cause, which is the reason, or the end for which the causality takes place. In this case, we could say that the final cause is whatever end Michelangelo intended by the construction of the statue. The statue may be an end in itself, or it may be a means to some ulterior end. Perhaps the sculptor wanted to earn some money, or to achieve immortality, or he simply acted on a whim. The final cause indicates the reason behind a particular event. Finally, there is the *formal* cause. Remember that a thing is always a composition of matter and form. The formal cause, then, is whatever makes a matter to be this particular thing. The formal cause makes the thing to be itself, by shaping the matter. Consider the historical David as an individual substance. As a combination of matter and form, David is a combination of the individual and the universal. Accounting for his particular individuality, according to Aristotle, is matter, which is the stuff David is made of. Conversely, the kind of thing that David is, which is a human being, is accounted for by the form which shapes this matter. This form could be called humanity. What is the causal form of the sculpture *David*? We might say it is the form of statue, or the essence of a statue. The form is not what makes *David* the particular statue that it is—the matter accounts for that—but it makes it a statue.

Now let us return to our question. Can any of these causalities be possessed by distinct triune persons in relation to creation? Rahner accepts that the efficient causality is always common to the divine persons. That is because an agent always acts through its essence, which is common and simple in the case of the Trinity. Material causation will be ruled out, since God cannot be the material cause of anything, himself being spiritual, and not capable of entering into any composition with anything. What about final causation? Well, in this case, the end for which God accomplishes anything is some idea in his mind, which, given divine simplicity, is the same thing as himself. So God can be taken to be the final cause of anything only taken essentially.

One kind of causality remains: formal causation. But Rahner knows there is a problem with this, just as there is a problem with material causation. A formal cause entails a composition with matter. That is to say that formal causes do not exist independently of the matter which they shape (unless one is a Platonist who accepts eternal forms). God is not matter, so he cannot be a material cause. But could God be a formal cause of some material thing? The difficulty here is that, as a formal cause, God would have to enter into composition with something. This has been consistently ruled out in Rahner's own tradition, for a variety of good reasons. Composition entails potentiality, because the form actualizes a potential in matter. The same block of marble can become both a urinal and a Michelangelo statue. But in God there is no potentiality, because that would entail that God can be improved on, or change for better or for worse. Moreover, in a form-matter compound, the form itself is dependent upon the matter in some sense. The form "humanity" depends on the idea of its fleshly matter, or the form "canine" depends on "four-leggedness" and so on. To say that God would be the form of some matter would make God himself depend in some form on that matter.

Rahner will not be fazed by these difficulties, however. Unfortunately, at this point we encounter a complexity that is unavoidable if we want to make sense of the historical and contemporary conversations about the divine missions. Rahner believes that, were the created term of a mission simply the common work of all the triune persons, that is of their common efficient causality, then there would be no genuine self-communication of the divine person through that medium. Rahner's complex solution is to say that in the created effect of a mission we have more than just the efficient divine causation but actually a kind of formal causation.

He argues that in the incarnation we have a precedent for a type of relation between a divine person and created reality that is more than just an appropriation. The human nature of Christ, as Chalcedonian Christology has emphasized, is without its own human hypostasis, that is, it is not personalized in a human way. The person of Christ is the eternal Logos, who has taken on flesh. It is precisely the person of the eternal Son that makes this human nature to be what it is, namely, the incarnate Son of God. But that is just what a formal cause does: it makes something to be the kind of thing it is. But in this case it is precisely the Son who makes this human nature to be what it is—since this nature does not have its own hypostasis. In humans, Rahner argues, it is precisely the human person that *actuates* the nature, that is, that actualizes this potentiality into the actual thing that exists. But in Christ there is no human person, so what actualizes this nature is precisely the Son of God. So the person of the Son is what Rahner, all too aware of the difficulties with formal causation in relation to God, is going to call a quasi-form of the human nature. The Son is what forms this human nature to be what it is.

The incarnation is a dogmatic instance, Rahner argues, of a type of relations that exist between specific divine persons and creation. In the indwelling of the Spirit we have another one, whereby the Spirit becomes what he calls the *quasi-form* of the human love, or some faculty in the human soul to which the Spirit is united.

With these moves, Rahner has shaken the foundations of the whole Augustinian-Thomist tradition of inseparable relations, appropriations, and sanctifying grace. He does not deny the rule of inseparable operations but restricts and clarifies its application to efficient causality. In that domain the doctrine of appropriations continues to apply. However, when it comes to the missions of the Son and the Spirit, visible and invisible, here we are in the domain of proper and not appropriated relations. It has to be noted at once that the tradition has always insisted that the missions themselves are not appropriated—when considered from the point of view of the procession—but proper. In a mission, Aquinas had argued, a person is truly given to us. But it is given to us through the created effect, and thus through some created grace—and this created term is commonly produced by the three. Rahner's rule has reversed the order of created and uncreated grace. It is not because of created grace that we have a relation to the uncreated person, as Aquinas had argued, but the opposite. Precisely because we are united to the divine person taken distinctly, we are sanctified. Aquinas had argued that sanctifying grace disposes us to receive the divine person. It prepares us for a spiritual vision, such as the one Augustine envisaged when he claimed that we are no longer in this world when we perceive the divine person. Rahner, and the theology that he has inspired, reverses the order: the divine person extends his quasi-form and communicates its own existence to creatures, as a result of which they are sanctified. To put it in admittedly imprecise terms, with Rahner, union with the divine persons is the way to sanctification; with the Augustinian-Thomist tradition, sanctification is the way to the union. We shall return to these matters downstream.

CONCLUSION

Our work thus far has revealed the fact that theological reflection on the mystery of the divine missions can make us alert to a number of facile preconceptions and mistakes. The notion of mission is a much weightier theological concept that should not be reduced to the simple notion of operations, or of a series of tasks. In its profound meaning, a divine mission indicates a divine self-communication, a divine in-reach into our world, without prejudice to either the divine being or indeed the created realities it affects. In the missions of the Son and the Spirit the persons are manifested by being united to creatures. This union is qualitatively superior to any theophanic conjuring of creatures. It is a constitutive and permanent union, whereby the creature is transformed, uplifted, whilst remaining the creature that it is. More specifically, as Aquinas has helped us realize, a mission represents the extension of a procession. Like a solar flare, it is a prolongation of the eternal dynamism of Father, Son, and Holy Spirit into creation, a new manner of divine existence in the world. And yet the unity and transcendence of God complicates the notion of a personal self-communication. God does not change in the mission, nor does he become dependent upon any created thing. And thus we are faced with the difficulty of accounting for the authenticity of this personal self-communication through a created term that is in fact the common work of the whole Trinity, and which cannot contain but is contained by God. We will revisit this difficulty as we go on to discuss specifically the visible and the invisible missions in the following two chapters.

2

THE VISIBLE MISSIONS OF THE SON AND THE SPIRIT

AS WE HAVE SEEN, THE MISSIONS EXTEND THE PROCESSIONS of the divine persons into the created world. They prolong the internal fruitfulness of the Trinity, the inexhaustible and perfect life of God into the world. They are like the solar storms that occasionally intensify for us the uninterrupted flow of light and life from the sun, and which often reach and disrupt the earth's magnetic fields. We need to understand the missions, as we have seen, in a way that is fitting with the divine transcendence and omnipresence to creation. In this chapter we are going to be contemplating two missions, of the Son and the Spirit. We will seek to understand them in their most ontological dimension, as temporal processions. We will interpret the life, ministry, death, resurrection, and ascension of Christ in this manner. It will be asked at which point does the Spirit's mission intervene and how the two missions are ordered to one another. In this chapter we will develop the argument that just as the procession of the Holy Spirit is consequent upon the begetting of the Son, the mission of the Spirit follows upon the mission of the Son. Pentecost thus naturally follows the ascension, and the Spirit can be fittingly called the Spirit of Christ, or the Spirit of the Son.

HYPOSTATIC UNION

We determined in the last chapter that a mission is an extension of the procession, such that the procession and the mission are not two different realities but one regarded from two different points of view. That means, as we shall discuss, that the general pattern of the missions will follow the pattern of the processions. In a mission, a procession finds another creature, which we will call *term*. A relationship of union takes place between the procession and the creature. The particular nature of such a union need not be identical for all missions, as different missions may be said to have different functions, just as the divine persons have different personal identities. Some of these unions, such as the one between the Son and his human nature, are irrevocable. In our view, the union resulting from the indwelling of the Holy Spirit is equally irrevocable. On the other hand, missions that are called *symbolic*, such as the baptismal dove, the tongues of fire, etc., although real missions, do not engage the divine person in a final union with these created natures. For this reason, Joseph Pohle rightly points out that "aside from the mission of the Incarnate Logos, an invisible mission as such invariably ranks higher than a visible mission, because it aims at the supernatural sanctification of the creature."[1] It may be said that in the incarnation, and in the invisible mission of the Son, a true and lasting union, though under various aspects, is brought about between the procession of the Son and a created term, such that it may be said that in these sundry ways the Son proceeds from the Father in the human nature of Christ and in the human heart.

The Nature of the Union

It will be important to identify the differences between the various unions with the divine persons in the visible mission of the Son and in the invisible missions of the Son and the Spirit. What kind of union is taking place in the incarnation of the Son? On this matter there are a variety of proposals, but they do not all assume the contours of conciliar Christology. It was Chalcedon in particular that stressed the anhypostatic-enhypostatic character of the human nature of Christ. To put it simply, it was accepted that Christ's human nature does not subsist in a human person, or rather it is not already personified prior to the assumption. Nestorius had argued that in Christ

---

1. Pohle, *Divine Trinity*, 250–51.

there are two hypostases, one human and another divine, and hence there was a union of grace between two persons, the Logos and Christ the son of Mary. The orthodox party recoiled against the monstrosity this entailed, a two-headed, two-personed savior, which destroys the unity of Christ as exhibited in the Scriptures. The settlement of the Chalcedonian council affirmed that the human nature is without its own proper hypostasis, but it becomes actualized in the hypostasis of the eternal Logos. That is, the human nature receives its existence from the Logos.

The religious significance of this move is immediately obvious. It implies that although this flesh is real human flesh, that his knowledge and soul are really human, these exist as the Son of God. Conversely, it means that the eternal Logos, whose existence is to be eternally proceeding from the Father, now exists in and through a human nature. Not that this would be an *esse secundarium*, a secondary existence of the Son, because in the Son essence and existence are the same and therefore necessary and nonseverable. Rather, now the subsistent relation that is the Son encompasses and permeates a human nature that retains all its properties and operations.

A Mixed Relation

It is traditionally said about this relation of union that it is a *mixed relation*, in that the created term of the union is altered and constituted by the relation itself, while the Son of God remains who he is. Thus, when we say that the procession and the mission are the same reality,[2] we must not suppose that this makes the eternal person depend on its relation to a creature. The Logos is not constituted in his very identity by the fact that he is incarnate and receives in time a human nature. The constitution and the motion always flow from the uncreated to the created. Bernard Lonergan appeals to the conceptuality of antecedent versus consequent conditions in order to explain that "the necessary external term is not a constitutive cause, but only a condition, and indeed a condition that is not prior or simultaneous, but consequent."[3] This distinction can be nicely illustrated when one considers a marathon runner who completes the marathon by running. In the process, however, her shoe soles wear out. Yet we cannot say that the destruction of her soles is the constitutive or antecedent cause of her completing the marathon. Rather, it was her running that makes it

2. Lombard, *Sentences: Book 1*, dist. 14, ch. 1.
3. Lonergan, *Triune God*, 441.

possible for her to complete the race. The effect upon her shoes is a necessary consequence of her running, not a condition of her running, and therefore not a condition of her completing the marathon.

Or, consider another scenario. A lifeguard notices a person drowning in the sea. He promptly jumps in the water, swims out to this person, grabs him and drags him back to shore. Necessarily the lifeguard will wet his swimsuit, cause ripples in the water, etc. But these additional events are not necessary in an antecedent sense for his saving the drowning person. They are necessary only in a consequent sense. They are only consequent conditions of his performing his saving activity.

Lonergan rightly understands that confusing the consequent and the constitutive (or antecedent) conditions in a divine mission will make the divine activity depend upon created conditions and therefore destroy divine aseity, simplicity, etc. Given that God's being is God's acting, the divine actions are not separate components of his existence, but they are his existence. But if this is true, and if the divine actions have created conditions of an antecedent kind, then the divine existence itself depends upon creation.

The idea that in a mission we have a mixed relation springs deep in the sources of the Christian tradition, East and West. It cannot be blamed on the Latin theology of *pure actuality*, which includes both the being and the activity of God—as opposed to the East, where it applies only to God's *super-essence*.[4] While it has been contested in modern theology, it has an impressive pedigree in a broad Christian orthodoxy. One metaphor often deployed to illustrate this was that of the iron placed in the fire. The fire heats the iron and makes it glow. Yet the fire itself does not change; it is not constituted as a fire by the iron. It does what it does; the iron changes and, in fact, begins to acquire some of the properties of the fire: heat and light.

This makes the religious significance of this model very clear. Human and created realities are brought into union with divine realities, and they are changed, transfigured. God himself does not change, evolve, or improve as a result of this. He is self-sufficient and omnipotent. The human nature that is brought into union with the Son does not supply him with additional active powers. As we shall see, the human nature of Christ and its operations do not enable God to save us any more than the iron enables the fire to burn, heat, or illuminate. It is precisely because creation has been drawn

---

4. We compare and contrast the Western and Eastern frameworks in Vidu, "Triune Agency, East and West."

into the self-sufficient and inextinguishable divine sun that it necessarily acquires certain properties of the sun.

Receiving the Existence of the Son

We have so far established that this relation is a mixed relation. It may be said that the whole Trinity creates the human nature of Christ to give it to the Son, who assumes it, conferring his existence as the one who comes from the Father to this human nature. It will follow that the very characteristic of this human nature is going to be a proper *receptivity*, mirroring the Son's eternal self-reception from the Father. If the procession of the Son is now extended to the human nature of Christ, this human nature will acquire the mode of existence of the Son. But this mode of existence is precisely one of coming from the Father and of receiving life from the Father (John 5:26). This mode of existence will now unfold on a human plane, in terms of the operations and properties of a human nature. Just as the iron does not stop being an iron and begins to exhibit the properties of the fire in a way that is consistent with its nature, so the human nature of Christ, without losing its natural properties, is raised above its natural capacities by its union with the Logos. We shall unpack this elevation of human existence to its theandric character in the next section.

We can now revisit Aquinas's claim that any of the other divine persons might have become incarnate.[5] In fairness to Aquinas, we have to note that he was merely rejecting the idea that the other divine persons either do not possess the same ability as the Son to become incarnate or, as we have seen with Augustine, that only the Son is intrinsically visible, as opposed to the Father, for example, who by definition is invisible. Each of the divine persons possesses the same set of capacities, since they share the same indivisible nature. The act of assuming a human nature is accomplished in virtue of the powers inherent in this divine essence. Thus, it must be said that the act whereby the human nature was united to the Son is of the whole Trinity. Father, Son, and Spirit draw this human nature towards the Son, while it is the Son only who receives it. Just like a magnet as a whole draws the needle and attaches it to one of the poles, which does not change by this activity, so the whole Trinity inserts the human nature specifically in the Father-Son relation, such that the Word now proceeds in history! And, just as the magnet is attached specifically to one of the poles and it receives

---

5. Aquinas, *ST* III, q. 3, art. 5, *sed contra*.

a specific electrical charge,[6] so the human nature is attached to the Son and receives the Son's own mode of existence. Moreover, to continue the analogy, just as the needle is elevated beyond its natural operation to become magnetized and to itself attract other metallic objects, so the human nature of Christ is now elevated beyond its natural operations to draw other human beings into its Father-Son relation (John 12:32). At the same time, the capacity of the human nature to draw does not reside in the human nature itself but, specifically, in the union with the Logos. For this reason, it is ultimately the Father who draws (John 6:44).

We have not discussed the metaphysics of this hypostatic union or Rahner's suggestion that what we have here is a *quasi-formal* communication of the existence of the Son. Our account of the union stresses that it is possible to speak about a true self-communication of the Son to the human nature of Christ, but without invoking the theologically questionable notion of quasi-formal causality. The mission implied by the hypostatic union is proper to the Son, as far as the union between the human nature and specifically the Son is concerned. But one need not go so far as to claim that the Son has now become the (quasi-) form of the human nature.[7] What the human nature does receive is the mode of existence and mode of action of the Son. The human nature is not formed by the Son (it does not take the Son's form) because the latter is a particular, and forms are universals and not particulars. Neither does the human nature become formed by the divine nature, since that would annul its humanity. What can be said, however, is that the human nature, whilst remaining human, receives the mode of existence and operation of the Son. That is, it receives the flow of divine life, as coming from the Father to the Son. The Logos remains distinct from his human nature, but now Christ's "human nature is always marked by the filial mode of existing proper to the divine Son who subsists in that human nature."[8] In Christ, human nature comes to participate in the divinity precisely at the point of sonship. The Logos extends his eternal sonship to include us. We are drawn by the whole Trinity to itself along this precise vector of sonship, through God's natural Son, Christ.

---

6. Here, it has to be noted the analogy fails, since the magnet receives the opposite charge from the pole.

7. For a particularly perceptive critique of Rahner's quasi-formality, see W. Hill, "Uncreated Grace."

8. Legge, *Trinitarian Christology of Thomas Aquinas*, 111.

Because the Son shares his mode of existence and operation with the human nature he has assumed, his sonship will be played out on the human scene. If we view the life of Christ, his human history, his temptation and obedience through the vantage point of the missions, then what we will find is the realization and expression in human categories of the eternal sonship of the Word.

THEANDRIC LIFE

Does the Spirit Come First? Spirit Christology

The construal proposed above has been seriously challenged in recent theology from the perspective of the Spirit's role in the incarnation. It is argued that the divinity of Christ should be construed not in the directly substantialist and ontological terms of Chalcedon but rather in terms of the presence of the Spirit in him. That is to say, Christ is divine not so much because he possesses from his conception a divine nature through hypostatic union. In the opinion of much modern theology since Adolf von Harnack, this type of Christology undermines the true humanity of Jesus. It fails to do justice to human properties he obviously possessed, such as ignorance, growth in knowledge and wisdom, etc. From so-called Spirit Christology, then, the alternative suggestion is that Christ's divinity must be understood precisely in terms of being full of the Holy Spirit.

This alternative can also be formulated from the perspective of the missions. Instead of arguing for a priority of the Son's mission, followed by his sending the Spirit on his own mission at Pentecost, the mission of the Spirit comes first. The reversal of the order of the missions has significant consequences, and we shall address them in the next chapter. But the idea can appear very plausible, unless certain important distinctions are born in mind.

We know, for example, that certain Old Testament believers are already filled with the Spirit. We can name the cases of the judges (Judg 6:34, 14:6), Saul (1 Sam 11:6), David (1 Sam 16:13), prophets (2 Chron 15:1), and others as well (Exod 31:3). More significantly, the Spirit appears to constitute and empower the very existence and life of Christ. He is present and instrumental in the very conception of Christ (Matt 1:18), the Spirit is present at Jesus's baptism, the Spirit prepares him for the temptation (Matt 4:1), etc.

If we are to take these instances seriously, then we should reconsider the traditional order of the missions, so certain theologians argue. Kathryn Tanner, for instance, suggests that we are to think of the missions as taking place not so much in a sequential order, separated by the ascension of Christ, but rather in interweaving fashion, whereby first we have the mission of the Spirit and then, immediately following, that of the Son.

There are several reasons why we should not embrace this alternative. On the one hand, if the missions mirror the processions, it would seem to entail a procession of the Son from the Father and the Spirit, *Spirituque*, or at least a procession from the Father via the Spirit. Tanner does not hesitate to bite this bullet and, with her, a number of other theologians, but the *Spirituque* procession of the Son continues to remain very much a minority position throughout the historic and global Christian tradition. Of course, some will counter that for precisely this biblical reason we should question the idea that the missions reveal the processions. We have already argued that if they do not reveal the processions, there is nothing else about the persons to be revealed by the missions. Moreover, the following argument seriously weakens the claim that the Spirit's mission (at conception) comes before the Son's.

A second difficulty is perhaps more damning. As we have seen, a mission entails a union between a divine person and a created term, or the extension of a procession to a created effect—because a mission is not simply a theophany but a divine self-communication. But, precisely for this reason, the work of the Spirit in the conception of Christ cannot be understood as a mission prior to the Son's mission. Before the mission of the Son, that is, before the union between the human nature and the Son, there was no such thing as the human nature of Christ. There is no created effect that could be united to the Spirit. The mission of the Spirit, in other words, cannot even get off the ground, not unless there is another created effect, not the humanity of Christ, to which it becomes united. If we are not careful here, we can easily imply a Nestorian scheme whereby humanity already exists and is indwelt by the Spirit. Alternatively, we might say that, even though the created effect does not exist, it comes to exist at the time of the Spirit's mission. In this case, however, perhaps even worse, we would have to affirm an incarnation of the Holy Spirit.

It may still be argued that the Spirit's mission is not in the sense of a union with the human nature of the Son, but rather a mission to Virgin Mary. In this case, the term of the Spirit's mission pertains to Mary herself.

We hesitate to draw this conclusion, for various reasons. John the Evangelist comments that "the Spirit was not" (John 7:39, author's translation) before Christ had been glorified and ascended. Any claim that the Spirit was given in a manner different from his Old Testament presence threatens the uniqueness of the Pentecostal dispensation of the Spirit. While Mary certainly was the recipient of an operation appropriated to the Holy Spirit, which is in fact the common triune act resulting in the creation of the human nature of the Son, this should not be understood as a mission in the sense we have defined.

The further difficulty apparently posed by the presence of the Spirit in Old Testament saints and in the conception of Jesus is much more correctly resolved by distinguishing between actions and missions. On these occasions we witness the operation of the whole Trinity, appropriated to the Spirit specifically, and not a mission *strictu sensu*. This is precisely what Augustine has in mind when he considers the divine theophanies. These take place not by way of a self-communication of the persons but rather by creature control.

The Spirit does sanctify and empower the humanity of Christ but not from a position of hypostatic union with it or any part of it. Only the Son assumes the human nature to himself. Humanity thus enters into the trinitarian life precisely at the point of the Son. It is precisely the Father-Son relation which is first opened up to it. This is not to say that humanity remains at that level. Quite the opposite. The gateway into the Trinity is sonship, the Logos. Christ is the sheep's gate (John 10:7). But since the processions are intrinsically and necessarily united to one another, from this port of entry, we are then irradiated by the other procession, of the Spirit. And by being so embraced by the "magnetic" field of Son and Spirit, we are raised to be with the Father as well.

Tanner does capture very well this dynamic. In the missions, the processions remain unaltered, the intra-trinitarian movement remains what it is, only this time they take "humanity along for the ride."[9] The created effect is not only attached to a particular trinitarian "pole," but consequently it begins to channel the other trinitarian relations. Only, as Tanner so aptly explains, what takes place instantaneously in the transcendent life of God is now played on in time and in a situation of human sin and brokenness. The uncreated energies of God begin to permeate the humanity of Jesus and transform it gradually, elevating it above its natural operations and

9. Tanner, *Christ the Key*, 145.

powers. As Dumitru Stăniloae, the Romanian Orthodox theologian, put it, Christ's humanity, specifically his body, becomes gradually transparent to the Spirit. The reason this does not take place instantaneously is because, unlike the hypostatic union, whereby the humanity of Christ is actuated as precisely the person of the Logos, this humanity remains what it naturally is; its transformation follows and respects its natural and temporal dynamism. The Holy Spirit is assimilated into the humanity of Christ gradually, even as the latter already possesses him in virtue of being the eternal Son in perichoresis with the Father and the Spirit. This is precisely what we may now observe in the life of Jesus.

Christ's Two Operations: Divine and Human

Let us continue along with our logic of the mission: in the incarnation the procession of the Son has been historicized and temporalized. The Son now is begotten from the Father not only before all time, but in time. Resulting from this is a human nature that now has the mode of existence of the Son and the Son's mode of operation. Now, the mode of operation of the Son does not abolish the human nature's original and natural operation! Orthodox Christology has insisted that in Christ there are two wills and two operations. Were the human nature without its own will and operation, it would be a mere abstraction. The Son has assumed a human nature that has its own intrinsic movement. What are some of these natural operations? Hunger, for example, thirst; the operations of the intellect, such as knowledge, memory; physical operations, such as moving one's body, breathing, etc. All of these the Son now does in virtue of having a human nature. Here is Leo the Great's explanation of how each nature acts in cooperation with the other: "For each form does what is proper to it with the co-operation of the other; that is the Word performing what appertains to the Word, and the flesh carrying out what appertains to the flesh. One of them sparkles with miracles, the other succumbs to injuries."[10] Many scholars agree that Leo disjuncts rather too clearly between the human operations and the divine operations. Much better is the formulation of Pseudo-Dionysius the Areopagite: "It was not by virtue of being God that he did divine things, not by virtue of being a man that he did what was human, but rather, by the fact of being God-made-man he accomplished something new in our

---

10. Leo the Great, "Letter XXVIII," 40.

midst—the activity of the God-man."[11] Maximus the Confessor continues the same idea: "As man, being by nature God, he acts humanly, willingly accepting the experience of suffering for our sake. And it is again made clear that as God, who is human by nature, he acts divinely and naturally exhibits the evidence of his divinity."[12]

John of Damascus often deploys the imagery of a flaming sword, hearkening back to our image of the iron brought into the fire. The flaming sword has two operations, that of cutting and burning. These are distinct and pertain to the two natures that are united: fire and iron. To cut naturally belongs to the iron or steel and not to the fire, while to burn naturally belongs to the fire and not to the metal. And yet the two operations are working inseparably.

The hypostatic union has brought about such a blessed conjunction of operations in the unity of the person of the eternal Logos, that everything that the human nature does and suffers, it suffers and does as God; and everything that God does, he does as man. The operator of all of Christ's operations is the whole Trinity, from whom come the efficient energy moving and instrumentalizing his human operation. The natural operation of his human nature, on the other hand, belongs exclusively to the Son, since the humanity subsists exclusively in him. The inseparable operation of the Trinity, which exists in its threefold modality and modes of action, and not three separate actions, or agents, is now channeled through the humanity of Christ and its own natural activity. It is our argument that the human operation and the human will of Christ are itself perfected in the process. His human nature is increasingly deified, or made transparent to the Spirit. This is a process entirely driven by the eternal Logos and thus by the whole Trinity.

Gradual Deification of Christ's Humanity

Let us think for a moment about Christ's temptation in the wilderness. We know that Christ was tempted in all things like us (Heb 4:15). But does Christ's undergoing temptation have a mere demonstrative purpose? It may be argued that, since Christ was the eternal Son of God, the temptation was not in fact experienced as such, in which case we may rightly wonder what use it might be to us that he has been so tempted? Rather, as Hebrews puts it,

11. Denys, *Pseudo-Dionysius*, epistula 4.
12. Maximus, "Opusculum 7," 84C.

he is able to sympathize with our weakness. The suggestion made by certain theologians that Christ has assumed a fallen human nature,[13] yet without sin, might save the authenticity of the wilderness temptations. Christ, in this scenario, assumes not an ideal pre-fall humanity, but one that bears the ontological consequences of the first sin. If we understand sin to be not merely personal and systemic but also ontological, in the sense of the introduction of a predisposition in human nature away from its original end, God, such that "no one seeks for God" (Rom 3:11), it might be possible to interpret Christ's sympathizing with our weaknesses in this way. Namely, the Son assumes a human nature whose primary ontological orientation is away from God, towards created things, a disoriented intentionality. At no instant in Christ's human will, however, does this inheritance ever dominate his God-consciousness, as Schleiermacher calls it. Yet it is there.

It cannot be argued that without such a fallen (although sinless) human nature, Christ could not have been tempted, since Adam was tempted even while possessing a perfect human nature. Some have suggested, additionally, that to have assumed a pre-fall perfect human nature would entail that Christ does not actually heal our humanity as much as he starts a new one. We are not going to adopt either of these alternatives but stress that, in Christ, there is a gradual deification of his humanity, a growing in his humanity's capacity for the Spirit. There is, as George Maloney calls it, a stretching-out of the human being for God: "The sameness and stability of our love for God fills us with a restless motion, a stretching-out quality towards God, the unpossessable, that thrills us because we know that, try as we may, we can never exhaust this richness."[14]

In this way we can account for the obvious development of Christ's humanity and thus perhaps satisfy some of the desiderata of a Spirit Christology. He "increased in wisdom and in stature and in favor with God and man" (Luke 2:52). It may be asked how this gradual deification is consistent with the claim of Aquinas and others that Christ already possesses the beatific vision. But Scripture itself claims, again in Hebrews (2:10), that Christ was made perfect by God through suffering; and, in Hebrews 5:8 the same Jesus "although he was a son, he learned obedience through what he suffered." Thus, whether or not Christ possesses the beatific vision as man from the very beginning, this must be consistent with his growth in wisdom and with his perfecting through suffering.

---

13. For an excellent analysis of the problem, see Crisp, "Did Christ Have."
14. Maloney, *Inward Stillness*, 87–88.

A certain slide towards adoptionism has proven to be quite irresistible for some theologians, partly on the basis of Philippians 2:6–11 ("bestowed on him the name that is above every name") but also Romans 1:4 ("appointed Son of God" [NIV]). Orthodoxy will not find these readings acceptable, however. The sonship of Christ is not something that is acquired; it is not an existential achievement but an ontological and metaphysical ground for his human existence. As we have pointed out, in a mission, the created effect is not a constitutive or antecedent cause but only a consequent cause. Christ learns obedience; he is perfected through suffering; he grows in wisdom, knowledge, and favor, not in order that he might become the Son, but precisely because he is the Son! The human nature is the instrument of his divinity. It is the Son who is wielding the flaming sword, so to speak. The eternal Son is acting through his humanity for us.

The procession is unfolding on the human plane, respecting the integrity of the humanity. This, too, is what explains the human obedience of the Son. We have to resist an Arian inference from the obedience of the Son to an ontological subordination of the Son to the Father. Not much better would be the so-called EFS (Eternal Functional Subordination) position, which only briefly dazed a number of evangelical theologians in the 2010s. Within the Trinity there can be no subordination of any kind, since there are not diverse substances but one substance, which has one will, one power, and one intellect. Everything except for the relations of origin is shared within the Trinity.

That said, there is a certain irreducible *taxis* within the Trinity, a certain flow of life from the Father to the Son, and then from the two to the Holy Spirit. This order is not subordination, for it is the very same life and power and will of the one God. At precisely this point we see the benefit of the conceptuality of missions: as this eternal *taxis* unfolds in the economy in and through the will and operations of a human nature, it translates as obedience. The eternal receptivity, which is the eternal Son, when expressed through the assumed human nature, becomes obedience, for there is a real substantial distinction between the divine and the human nature. One can and must say that the incarnate Son is obedient, because he now possesses a different nature, with its own will, power, and intellect. For that same reason, the Son can do only what he sees the Father doing (John 5:19); for that same reason, Christ submits his will to the Father—because his human will *is* distinct from the Father's, unlike his divine will; and, for that reason,

Christ's human knowledge does not appear to be on a par with his divine omniscience (Matt 24:36; Mark 13:32).

Does the Cross Break the Trinity?

Regarding the cross with the conceptual tools provided by the doctrine of the divine missions may lead to some valuable takes on the doctrine of the atonement. We have enunciated the principle that in a mission the created effect is only a consequent, rather than a constitutive, condition. This means that the human activity and passivity of Christ (his life of obedience and his sacrificial death) cannot be taken as enabling the ultimate divine salvific action in any way. The Son of God is not enabled to heal or forgive by his uttering audible sounds: "Your faith has saved you; go in peace" (Luke 7:50). Neither can it be said about the suffering of Christ that it disposes the Father to forgive, when otherwise he may have been unable or unwilling to. As long as we affirm that Father, Son, and Spirit share one divine will and the same divine power, we cannot say that one of them is unable to do a certain operation until another one completes his own operation. The Son cannot be said to enable the Father to forgive. The Son's power of forgiveness is the same as the Father's power of forgiveness—just as any other power is identical between the three.

What, then, of the death of Christ? From the standpoint of the mission of the Son, the Son expresses and lives out his sonship precisely as man, taking to himself the entire human condition, possibly including our fallen human nature. His receptivity is lived out precisely as a human obedience, yet not one in the abstract but precisely in the face of death. Moreover, it may be said that the death Jesus dies is a penal death, as "the wages of sin is death" (Rom 6:23). The eternal Son steps into our very penal condition, he lives a human life, culminating in a death in God-forsakenness.

Jesus's cry of dereliction (Mark 15:34; Matt 27:46) may not be understood, as Moltmann and McCormack do,[15] as a rupture in the very being of God. Projecting this death into the very being and existence of God may help us arrive at a more sympathetic, empathic view of God. But, as Bruce Marshall has demonstrated, this is ultimately either unsatisfactory or disingenuous. Let us dwell on this familiar petition in modern theology, viz.,

---

15. McCormack, "Ontological Presuppositions of Barth's Doctrine"; Moltmann, *Crucified God*.

that suffering and death must affect the very being of God and should not be quarantined to the human nature of Christ. Let us assume for a moment that God truly gives himself over to the experience of death or, as Moltmann puts it, that God truly experiences the loss of his Son. For starters, a quick trinitarian caution is in order: in classical trinitarianism, such a break in the Father-Son relation is unimaginable, precisely because they are constituted by their relations. If the relation is broken or destroyed or annulled in some way (whatever that may mean in God), then the persons themselves are annihilated. In which case one may rightly wonder, who is left to raise Christ from the dead?

Now, of course, Moltmann has already abandoned classical (or Latin) trinitarianism. But there are severe problems even from the standpoint of his own social trinitarianism. If God truly gives himself over to the experience of suffering, in the same way that humans do, then—unless he is disingenuous—God faces the real risk of being overcome by suffering. We may rightly ask, in virtue of what does God overcome death and suffering? Is his victory a contingent one or a necessary victory? If it is contingent, we should rightly shudder, for away goes all our assurance of salvation and God's care for the world. What is to prevent God from eventually giving up on all the pain in the world? What is to prevent him from falling into an incurable depression, for example? On the other hand, if God's victory over death wasn't just God winging it but a necessity, because he was God, after all, then can it still be said that he has truly given himself over to the experience of suffering?

Does the Cross Move God?

It seems clear to us that the comforts provided by Moltmann's passible God are only temporary, and they do not measure up to the requirements of a Christian theism. We want to claim, on the contrary, that death and suffering have no chance against God. Precisely for that reason, God takes them to himself—in the human nature of Christ—so that they might be extinguished. Here God acts precisely as God, retaining his divine prerogatives and yet exercising them in and through a passible human nature. But God does not save because he incorporates suffering in his divine life; feminist theologians are rightly troubled by this. Just as the marathonist doesn't win the race because she wears out her shoe soles, God doesn't redeem us because he suffers. Rather, he suffers because he redeems, just as the runner wears out her shoes because she is competing in a race!

The doctrine of the divine missions brings out the unitive character of redemption. For God to redeem is precisely for him to extend the existence and life of his Son, the very prototype of humanity, himself the perfect Image of the Father, to human beings. The preference for an ontological language (union, deification) does not render obsolete the more forensic and legal aspects of redemption. But the tendency to order the legal to the ontological when theology foregrounds the missions must be acknowledged and perhaps even embraced. We shall reckon with some of these aspects in the next chapter, as we consider justification, sanctification, and deification.

It is not the death of Christ itself that is salvific anymore than it is the pain inflicted by the surgeon that causes the healing. The saving power of the death of Christ comes from the power that goes through it, which is the one power of God. Since death reigns over the kingdom of men, it was death that he had to taste as well. Death had to be assumed, just like a rational soul had to be assumed. Not because death is a part of human nature—it is not—but because it is part of human existence, part of our lot.

From the sowing of the Logos into this mortal soil springs to new life a new Adam, a new line of humanity. Scripture speaks of this in terms of the seed that must first go into the ground and then germinate into a new life (1 Cor 15:38–44). In the resurrection, Christ has defeated death, and it no longer reigns (Rom 5:17; 6:9). Nor are we to fear death or even view it as penal. Its sting is gone (1 Cor 15:55), for Christ has gone through it in a way that we do not have to. Christ has experienced death as a true God-forsakenness. This alone explains his agony before the cross. It is the human experience of God-abandonment that he submits himself to. He goes through this kind of death so that we won't have to. This is penal substitution. But he also goes through death in the same way that we shall have to: victoriously.

An ontologically-biased approach to the cross will not seek a constitutive logic, legal or otherwise, of atonement, bound up in some calculus that allows God to redeem. The cross does not move God. Rather, because God lay stretched on the cross, the cross acquires its power. Because God dies (in Christ's human nature), death is defanged. It is God and God alone who allows himself to redeem. No economy of exchange is discernible here.[16]

16. An "economy of exchange" typically refers to those models of the atonement that stress the divine justice in forgiving sins by inflicting a punishment on the Son. Such

And yet this sheer victorious passage of the Son through death best conveys its intelligibility in language that is partly legal: we are redeemed, adopted, justified.

Death is not an end in itself of the incarnation but its natural terminus, without which the incarnation would not have its redemptive power. The uncreated energies of the Son, united to human nature, suffuse every aspect of his human existence, every activity and every passion, including the ultimate passion, death. But the logic of the mission is also a logic of transfiguration. Just as the iron is made to glow in the fire, so the humanity of Christ is deified and transfigured in its passage through life and Sheol.[17] For this reason, Jesus associates his death with glorification in John 12:24. The new humanity that Christ fashions out of the old has already gone through death; it has already defeated it in the resurrection and therefore is no longer mortal.

It is possible to understand the saving death of Christ as the culminating point whereby the transforming energies of the Word *transfigure* the humanity of Christ. The human sonship of the Word is at this point completely realized, completely permeating the humanity of Christ, making it transparent to the Spirit. This brings us to the culminating moment of the Son's human mission, which is precisely his resurrection and ascension. Far from being a mere happy ending to a glorious mission, these moments are the pivotal point whereby the Spirit emerges from the humanity of Christ. At this point *the mission of the Son introduces the mission of the Spirit.*

ASCENSION AND PENTECOST

This brings us to the visible mission of the Holy Spirit at Pentecost. The argument we have been developing is that in a mission, a procession unfolds externally and temporally through a created effect. With the exception of the symbolic missions, perhaps improperly called missions, the created effect is transfigured and elevated beyond its natural operations, as it becomes engaged in the flux of trinitarian life at the point of the person who is

---

models are critiqued because they appear to condition the divine forgiveness upon something being provided in exchange. See, for example, Gorringe, *God's Just Vengeance*. We have explored several related theologies of the cross in Vidu, *Atonement, Law, and Justice*.

17. For an excellent contribution to the theology of Holy Saturday, see Emerson, "He Descended to the Dead." Although we dissent from its trinitarian conclusions, we should also mention Balthasar's *Mysterium Paschale*. For a counterweight to Balthasar, see Pitstick, *Light in Darkness*.

sent. But because the persons are indivisible and mutually indwelling each other, the mission itself begins to channel the other processions. Thus, the human nature of Christ shows the Father ("Whoever has seen me has seen the Father" [John 14:9]), but it also begins to channel the Spirit, as Christ himself becomes full of the Spirit.

Why Must the Son First Ascend?

Viewed from the missions, the coming forth of the Spirit at Pentecost only after the ascension of Christ begins to make more sense. The *staggering of the missions* has been something of a puzzle for this traditional ordering of the missions. Why must the Spirit's mission commence only after Christ has departed? John has Jesus explain to the disciples that "it is to your advantage that I go away, for if I do not go away, the Helper will not come to you. But if I go, I will send him to you" (John 16:7; cf. 7:39). Luke ties the Pentecostal outpouring with Jesus's receiving the Spirit from the Father: "Being therefore exalted at the right hand of God, and having received from the Father the promise of the Holy Spirit, he has poured out this that you yourselves are seeing and hearing" (Acts 2:33). To say that Christ receives the Spirit only upon his ascension is surprising in light of John 20:22, where he breathes on the disciples and tells them "receive the Holy Spirit" prior to the ascension.

Theologians have puzzled over the conditioning of the Spirit's mission upon the completion of the Son's. One unsatisfactory explanation was to interpret the reception of the Spirit from the Father as a *reward* for the completed mission.[18] This fails to take into account the fact that Christ already has the Spirit to bestow during his earthly life, or at the very least after the resurrection. Additionally, such an explanation perceives the Spirit to be *extrinsic* to Christ and in particular extrinsic to the humanity of Christ. But if the Spirit is extrinsic to the humanity of Christ itself, the union which the Spirit is said to create between the believer and Christ (see ch. 3) will be entirely extrinsic, making it hard to understand how Christ will be with us forever, after his ascension, precisely through the Holy Spirit.

The logic of the missions shows a better way forward. Because in the mission of the Son the human nature of Christ is united to the Word, it is engaged in such a way that it begins to externally *spirate* the Holy Spirit.

---

18. For example, Witsius, *Sacred Dissertations on the Apostles' Creed*, 2:227; Smeaton, *Doctrine of the Holy Spirit*, 134.

That is, the Holy Spirit not only proceeds internally, from the shared love of the Father and the Son, but externally through the incarnate Son's returning everything to the Father. Just as, in the bosom of the Trinity, the Spirit is the shared love between the Father and the Son, the Spirit proceeds outwards when the Son fully reciprocates and returns the Father's love. But now, as we have seen, this return of the Father's love by the Son is in the medium of a fallen and suffering world and in the face of death. Christ's love for the Father is perfected through suffering. Only when perfected in this way, or, as Stăniloae has put it, only when he has been made fully transparent to the Spirit, only then is the humanity of Jesus capable of breathing out the Spirit.

In this way it may be said with Aquinas that Christ merits the Spirit, not in a legalist sense, but rather in the sense that he becomes *capacious* for the Spirit. As we have seen in the last section, none of this means that Christ did not already have the Spirit. But his divine operation, which includes the agency of the Spirit, gradually energizes the natural human operation, and this takes time—because God respects the integrity of the natures he assumes. Neither can the obverse be said, namely that the sonship of Christ is only gradually realized through the Spirit's work.[19] But there is a certain expression and manifestation of the sonship of Christ, ontologically secured from the hypostatic union onwards, and yet existentially manifested in the gradual deification of Christ's human nature. As Schillebeeckx put it, "The actual prerequisite for the sending of the Spirit of salvation is therefore Christ's obedience and attachment to the Father."[20] As we have seen, Christ's obedience just is the human correspondent of the eternal receptivity of the Son.

The Spirit Comes From and Mediates Christ's Humanity

The implications are weighty. The Spirit comes down to us not simply from the divinity of Christ, and thus not simply as an act of the whole Trinity, but from the humanity of Christ, having already permeated it and thus having himself been *shaped* by it for us. As Legge observes with regard to Aquinas, the humanity of Christ has not only a ministerial causality in the sending of the Spirit but a certain efficient causality as well. Christ gives us the Spirit without measure because he has the Spirit without measure, as John 1:16 declares: "From his fulness we have all received, grace upon grace." This

---

19. Schillebeeckx, "Ascension and Pentecost."
20. Schillebeeckx, "Ascension and Pentecost," 352.

results from the manner in which the created effect (in this case the human nature of Christ) participates in the processions (in this case receiving sonship from the Father and, respectively, giving spiration to the Spirit). This results from the classical (Western) arrangement of the processions: the Father donates his own being to the Son, who receives it; the Son and the Father donate the divine being to the Spirit. Within the immanent Trinity, the Spirit's personhood is a function of his spiration from the Father and the Son. In light of the missions, his personhood is manifested through Christ's humanity. Since the Spirit is not incarnate, there is no created effect to be united specifically to him; thus he is manifested as the radiation of the Son's own humanity.

This helps us understand why the Spirit can unite us to Christ: because he is intrinsically shaped for us by Christ. He does not merely reflect the Spirit for us (ministerially), but he also inflects him for us (efficiently). That is to say that the Son modulates the Spirit through his own humanity for us. This, of course, assumes that the internal, intra-trinitarian procession of the Spirit is itself shaped by the Son. Naturally, then, the external procession of the Spirit will be shaped by the incarnate Son as well. Paul in particular likes to bring out that the Spirit we have received is the "Spirit of Christ" or the "Spirit of his Son" (Rom 8:9; Gal 4:6; Phil 1:9). In Romans 8:9–10, Paul writes, "You, however, are not in the flesh but in the Spirit, if in fact the Spirit of God dwells in you. Anyone who does not have the Spirit of Christ does not belong to him. But if Christ is in you, although the body is dead because of sin, the Spirit is life because of righteousness." Not only does the Spirit function between Christ and the believer in a way similar to the mediation of God's presence by the Spirit in the OT, but Christ is said to be present himself through the Spirit.

This *Christoformation* of the Spirit helps us affirm a strongly realist sense of the presence of Christ with the church. The Spirit who mediates Christ's presence is not merely a delegate but is precisely the Spirit breathing out through Christ's humanity and, even more specifically, the Spirit that bursts forth *e latere Christi*, from the side of Christ, as the river of living water. We can thus speak not only of a "dynamic identification"[21] between the Spirit and Christ but of a particular ordering and shaping of the Spirit by Christ. Speaking of a *dynamic identification* prevents a modalist confusion of the two persons, such as may seem encouraged by 1 Corinthians

---

21. For an excellent exegetical analysis of the relation between the risen Christ and the Spirit, see Fatehi, *Spirit's Relation to Risen Lord*.

15:45 ("the first Adam became a living being; the last Adam, a life-giving spirit"), which apparently emphasizes the identity between Christ and the Spirit.

The ultimate benefit of the Son's mission, then, is precisely the Spirit's mission. Together, the Son and the Spirit are the two outstretched hands of the Father, gathering creation and humanity back to himself. The port of entry for our return is precisely the humanity of Christ. In this humanity, which is the redeemed and transfigured Adamic humanity, we have all the benefits of salvation. In this humanity our sins are forgiven, our penalty paid. More importantly, however, in this humanity we find the Spirit, who writes the law upon our new hearts, hearts of flesh. The inseparability of the two missions is essential, but so is the order of the missions. The Spirit is ordered to Christ, just as he proceeds from the Son and the Father. The Spirit will not only remind us of Christ (John 14:26; 15:26; 16:8–14), but he will take from what is Christ's and make it known (John 16:15).

The visible mission of the Spirit completes the visible mission of the Son, but it also inaugurates the Son's invisible mission. John Zizioulas puts it somewhat starkly: "Now if becoming history is the particularity of the Son in the economy, what is the contribution of the Spirit? Well, precisely the opposite: it is to liberate the Son and the economy from the bondage of history. If the Son dies on the cross, thus succumbing to the bondage of historical existence, it is the Spirit that raises him from the dead. The Spirit is the *beyond* history, and when he acts in history he does so in order to bring into history the last days, the eschaton."[22]

This helps us understand why it is for our benefit that Christ goes away. Had Christ stayed, his presence would have been circumscribed to a particular location, as one having a body. Having ascended, and having thus become for us a life-giving Spirit, he is present repletely, everywhere.[23] As Paul puts it in Ephesians 4:10, "He who descended is the one who also ascended far above all the heavens, that he might fill all things." Christ's ascension is not in fact a departure but an even deeper lodging into the depth of all things. This brings us full circle: just as in a mission we must not imagine an ontological descent, a taking leave of heaven by a divine person, or an arrival to a new place, neither must we assume that in ascending

---

22. Zizioulas, *Being as Communion*, 130.

23. This presence need not imply the ubiquity of the body of Christ, which would appear to threaten his bodily nature. However, we may think of the body of Christ as having ascended to another "dimension," so to speak, from whence all spaces are accessible.

back, the person leaves this place or returns to a sender. The language of descent and ascent is perspectival. Its truth pertains most directly to the transformation that takes place in the created reality. In being sent, the person becomes manifest and united with the creature; in returning, the creature makes its way back to its ultimate destiny. In this way, the missions are but the vectors for the return of humanity to God. But the external missions, in and of themselves, are insufficient. For that reason we now turn to the invisible missions of the Son and the Spirit.

CONCLUSION

Once we realize that a divine mission is not simply a specific set of tasks and operations but rather the very communication of a divine mode of existence to a creature, we have to be on guard against facile misinterpretations of the various events comprising these missions. These events exist because there exists a divine mission; they are not antecedent to it. The same goes for the suffering and death of Christ. They do not unlock some hidden capacity in God, since it is the whole of the Godhead who supplies the energy and will for them. The very life of Christ is theandric because it subsists in the person of the Word, whose operation moves it. His human nature and operations, however, remain genuine and real, but not because they could have a human personal center. It is the Word himself who actualizes this human nature and operations and, in the process, communicates to them his personal property. The Son's eternal receptivity unfolds historically in the form of his human obedience of the Father. But there's more: the Son's mission not only mirrors his being begotten of the Father; it also ushers in the Spirit's own mission. Their missions are ordered to one another in the same manner as their processions. Ascension is the presupposition of Pentecost because it represents the historical summation of the Son's mission, the completed return of his love to the Father. It may then be said that the ultimate outcome of the Son's mission is the Spirit's own mission.

3

THE INVISIBLE MISSIONS

THE CHRISTIAN DOCTRINE OF SALVATION, TAKEN IN ITS MOST ontological aspect, affirms that the Christian enters into the trinitarian fellowship and that the triune persons themselves come to exist afresh in him, as Jesus promises (John 14:23): "If anyone loves me, he will keep my Word, and my Father will love him, and we will come to him and make our home with him." The indwelling of the divine persons of the Son and the Spirit is called the doctrine of the invisible missions. Whilst the reality of the missions is universally affirmed, the precise formality of the missions has been debated, especially in Catholic theology, since about the beginning of the twentieth century. The question of formality, or the manner and form in which the persons indwell, naturally arises from the assumption of the ontological difference and transcendence of the divine persons. We will canvas the various options and express our own preference. Related to the problem of formality is the trinitarian issue of whether in the invisible missions there are relations to the distinct divine persons. Do we have, for instance, the Holy Spirit himself or only his gifts? We shall take up this notion under the rubric of the finality of the invisible missions. These first three subheadings, on the reality, formality, and finality of the missions, complete our analysis of the notion of invisible missions, after which we proceed to a set of implications for ecclesiology and missiology. We will consider in which sense may we take the church to be a continuation of the divine mission? To address this question comprehensively, we shall engage with recent work on *missio Dei*.

THE REALITY OF THE INVISIBLE MISSIONS

It poses no special difficulty to say that the Christian is indwelt by the two persons of the Son and the Spirit. Jesus promises to send his Spirit, the Helper or Comforter, upon his ascension. The reception of this Spirit is also associated with power (Acts 1:8), which comes *upon* us, something visibly manifested through the tongues of fire (Acts 2:3). The invisible presence of the Spirit, however, entails an interior presence, for "the Spirit of God dwells in you" (Rom 8:9; cf. Rom 8:11; 1 Cor 3:16; 6:19; John 14:17). It is not the Spirit alone who indwells believers, for the Son also does. Paul explains that Christ dwells in our hearts by faith (Eph 3:17; Rom 8:10; 2 Cor 13:5; Col 1:27). The two missions are thus indivisible, even though they are ordered according to the pattern of the processions, as was the case with the visible missions.

The ordering of the missions to one another is first seen in how the mission of the Spirit is to unite us to Christ and, therefore, to inaugurate the invisible mission of the Son. Just as visibly the Son inaugurates the Spirit's external mission, invisibly the *reditus* of creatures backtracks the order of the visible missions. Visibly the Son is first sent, and then the Spirit. Invisibly, it is the interior work of God, appropriated to the Spirit,[1] that draws us to Christ, for no one is able to confess Christ's lordship except by the Holy Spirit. It is the operation of the Spirit, or appropriated to the Spirit, that draws us into the mission of the Son. It is the Spirit who is sent to convict the world of sin, righteousness, and judgment (John 16:8), all in relation to Christ.

We hesitate to say specifically that the invisible mission of the Spirit comes before the invisible mission of the Son, for if the formality of the Spirit's mission is love and the Son's mission is knowledge, as we shall explain later, love cannot come before knowledge. Love implies knowledge, even if knowledge does not necessarily imply love. Nevertheless, the drawing of persons into the love of God is correctly appropriated to the Spirit, and yet it must be clear that it is an operation. Only when this operation is completed, that is, only when this drawing becomes a union, can we speak of a mission *strictu sensu*. When such a person is united to the Trinity, it is precisely in the person of the incarnate Son that it is united, and from this

---

1. Here we might say that this work is only appropriated to the Holy Spirit. Thus, strictly speaking, this is not a mission, for one cannot love what one doesn't know.

union (whose form is knowledge and faith), the love (which is the formality of the Spirit's mission) springs forth.

Paul clearly associates our sonship with Christ's own natural sonship to the Father and with the giving of the Holy Spirit. We have received the Spirit of God's Son because we are sons (Gal 4:6). It is clear from this as well that the logical order is, first, sonship and, second, the reception of the Holy Spirit. It must be stressed, however, that these are not two moments separated in time, for it is impossible to have an indwelling[2] of the Son (and thus sonship) without also loving the Son and the Father and the Spirit.[3]

In Romans 8 Paul explains how Christ fulfills what was impossible for the law to do, weakened as it was by the flesh. The sent Son fulfills the "righteous requirement of the law" in us, who walk according to the Spirit and not the flesh. If we have the Spirit, we are no longer in the flesh but in the Spirit. "Anyone who does not have the Spirit of Christ does not belong to him" (Rom 8:9). The close association between the Spirit operative in the life of Christ and Christ is most clearly demonstrated here. "All who are led by the Spirit of God are sons of God" (8:14). This Spirit is a "Spirit of adoption as sons, by whom we cry, 'Abba! Father!'" (8:15). Paul later goes on to explain that this was God's plan from the beginning, namely that the whole creation will be liberated from its enslavement to corruption and its futility, into the "freedom of the glory of the children of God" (8:21).

Being sons means we have access to the Father (Eph 2:18). While the Father is not said to be sent, he, too, is indwelling (John 14:23), and yet in the case of the Father, this indwelling is always mediated by the invisible missions of the Son and Spirit. It is through the Son that we see the Father, for example. As in the case of the two missions, the presence of the Father must be understood in a way consonant with his omnipresence. The Father is always present, but in the mission of the Son he is cognized, he becomes manifest to our knowledge. And yet it is the Son that is sent and not the Father. Thus the Father has no mission.

The new relationship into which we are engrafted is also "sealed" by the Spirit (Eph 1:13; 4:30). The Spirit's indwelling is not conditional upon

---

2. While the Scripture does not use the specific language of "indwelling" for the Son, but only for the Spirit (Rom 8:11), God himself has promised to dwell in the people and to walk among them (cf. 2 Cor 6:16). We are therefore applying "indwelling" to all the divine persons, noting that the form of each indwelling is distinct.

3. It does not mean that this love has to be of a cognitive kind; love must be broadly understood as attachment, and it must be inclusive of persons with impaired cognitive abilities.

our perfection, since he may be grieved, even while continuing to keep us sealed to Christ. The fact that it is the Spirit who seals us is not accidental, for if the Spirit is the love that binds the Father and the Son into their unbreakable union, then we are sealed into God with the ultimate metaphysical glue, such that "no one will snatch" us (John 10:28–29) from Christ. The Christian can place all his confidence in God, and the ground for this is the fact that "God's love has been poured into our hearts through the Holy Spirit who has been given us" (Rom 5:5). The bond between Father and the Son is the Holy Spirit as their common love. The bond between the believer and Christ is the same Spirit, poured into our hearts. We are bound to Christ by the ultimate love.

John (1 John 4:13) also affirms the same logical connection between our having Christ and the Spirit: "By this we know that we abide in him and he in us, because he has given us of his Spirit" (cf. also 1 John 3:24). He then goes on to speak about the love which we have received: "So we have come to know and to believe the love that God has for us. God is love, and whoever abides in love abides in God, and God abides in him" (1 John 4:16). On the basis of this close association between the Spirit and the love that God has poured into our hearts, a significant tradition will come to speak about Love as the precise formality of the Spirit's indwelling, as we will see presently.

Our incorporation into Christ and thus our adoption as sons by the Spirit engage the Christian in a process of sanctification as a result of his having died with Christ (Col 3:3). This transformation that we call sanctification does not take place immediately, even if we "have been filled by" Christ (Col 2:9) and "renewed in knowledge according to the image" of our Creator (Col 3:10). We are to "continue to live in Him, being rooted and built up in Him and established in the faith" (Col 2:6). As a result of having the Spirit, we are to walk by the Spirit, and not according to the flesh, following its desires (Gal 5). The indwelling persons bring about a change in dispositions, precisely the heart of flesh anticipated by the prophet Ezekiel (11:19; 36:26). The Spirit is also bearing fruit, as Paul explains in Galatians 5, in the form of new desires, "desires of the Spirit" (Gal 5:17).

Finally, the Spirit constitutes the new humanity of Christ, the new body of Christ, his church. By baptism we are incorporated in the ecclesial body of Christ (1 Cor 12:13), in which all ethnicity, class, and gender are subordinated to our common sonship (Gal 3:28; Eph 2:18; Col 3:11). By the indwelling of the Spirit we have become, individually (1 Cor 6:19) and corporately (1 Pet 2:5–9), his temples.

Here we have come to a crucial moment in our discussion of the indwelling missions. We have seen in previous chapters that, as a result of union with a procession, the created effect has access to the principle (or source) of the procession (i.e., to the Father in union with the Son), but that the created effect also gradually begins to share in the external procession of the third person—in the case of the Son's mission, the external procession of the Holy Spirit. It is not entirely without justification to say that something similar happens in the invisible mission of the Son as well. In the visible mission, not only is his human nature related to the Father in obedience, but his humanity also spirates the Spirit for us externally. In the invisible mission, likewise, our humanity is not only adopted into sonship, and thus sharing in the Son's relation to the Father, but our humanity may also be said to spirate, in an analogical way, the Spirit for others.

Jesus promises that "whoever believes in me, as the Scripture has said, 'Out of his heart will flow rivers of living water.'" He then clarifies that by these rivers he means the Holy Spirit, whom those who believed him were to receive (John 7:38–9). Note the duality here: the Spirit is both received by believers and flows out of believers, like rivers of living water. In keeping with the ontology of the missions, it must be made clear that believers do not make any constitutive contribution to the mission of the Spirit. That is, we have no control over the Spirit, who is not operating at our behest. And yet, the Spirit may allow himself to be inflected precisely by the human operations of those who receive him and then pass him on. This adaptation of the Spirit to the creature is in line with the Spirit's anonymity, his cloaking himself within the normal operations of the indwelt person, à la Romans 8.

This possibility is ecclesiologically significant. The Spirit, who has been sent to dwell in the church as in his temple, and in believers as well, may be said to instrumentalize the human operations of the church, or its apostles, or its members, to accomplish his operations in the world. When Jesus breathes out the Spirit upon his disciples in the days after his resurrection, he continues, "If you forgive the sins of any, they are forgiven them; if you withhold forgiveness from any, it is withheld" (John 20:23; cf. Matt 16:19; 18:18). The power of the Holy Spirit may be said to operate precisely through the instrumentality of the church and believers. This invites a consideration of ecclesiology precisely from the perspective of the continuing mission of the Son and the Spirit in it, a project that we will have to defer.

We have thus far established the reality of the invisible missions. We noted that both the Son and the Spirit are indwelling in believers, together with the Father, who is not sent but sends. The invisible missions are also indivisible, and yet they are ordered to one another. The Spirit's mission consists in his uniting us to the Son. Considering the formality of these missions will further illuminate their pattern.

THE FORMALITY OF THE INVISIBLE MISSIONS

To some it may seem as if asking this question is unnecessarily complicated. Aren't the persons present as themselves? In one sense, certainly, the persons are themselves present. But a quick glance back at our Flatland analogy will help us realize the importance of this question. Isn't the sphere present in Flatland? Surely it is, but is it present as itself, as a sphere? For the Flatlanders the sphere certainly does not retain its own form, since Flatland is not capable of containing such a form. In this case, the *formality* of the sphere's presence in Flatland is a circle. Because the two are ontologically different, it is impossible for a substance from a superior ontological domain to be present in another substance as itself, while it is certainly possible for inferior substances to be present as themselves to God. *God contains everything, himself not contained by anything.*

The Persons Are Assimilated into the Believer

Aquinas adopts this principle and gives it the following formulation: "Whatever is received into a thing is received according to the recipient's mode."[4] This is no gratuitous metaphysical restriction but rather an example of metaphysical respect for both the integrity of the receiving nature and, in this case, the transcendence of the divine nature. God most certainly fills everything by his immensity and power. But in the indwelling we are reckoning with a different mode of the divine presence than simply this presence by immensity, or the divine omnipresence. In this case, the presence of the divine persons is of a different kind, not simply a more intense kind. Rather, we are dealing with a kind of *assimilation* of the divine person into the creature, a permeation of the believer by the divine person, who is not merely omnipresent to him but rather penetrates the creature and

---

4. Aquinas, *In Sent* 1, dist. 17, in Aquinas, *On Love and Charity*, 10.

transforms it. The presence is, in other words, not merely sustaining, as in the case of omnipresence, but transforming. The creature and God are not merely juxtaposed; it is not merely God's repletive presence but a summoning presence, where the creature is called out to be itself in a higher mode.

Consider the magnet again. It may be said that the magnetic field fills the space in the vicinity of the magnet. The field is repletely present in, say, biological tissue. But (as far as we know) such tissue is not affected by the magnetic field itself. It is indifferent to it. However, in metallic objects, the magnetic field is not only repletely present, but it also beckons such creatures to itself and magnetizes them upon their union with it. Similarly, as Aquinas explains, in rational creatures there can be a special presence of the Trinity by knowledge and love, which are operations and habits of the creature that dispose it to be united with the Son and the Spirit, as we shall see.

The very nature of the indwelling relation, in other words, entails a sort of assimilation of the divine person into the creature. But the assimilation of one thing into another is not the simple presence of one thing in another. Take the example of a food item, say, an apple. The apple is not assimilated simply when it is present spatially within my body. The relationship is one of spatial inclusion, but only when the apple has become digested can it be said that it has become assimilated. In this case it can be said that the formality of the apple's assimilation into my body is tissues and fluids. Or, in photosynthesis, carbon dioxide and water are assimilated in the form of organic molecules. The analogy loses traction here, and it can mislead us into thinking that the divine person disappears as it becomes assimilated into the creature. This, of course, is nonsensical, for divinity cannot disappear or change. Just as the fire becomes assimilated into the iron without it disappearing, so the divine person permeates the creature, without changing.

Sanctifying Grace

Aquinas, following Augustine, insists that the manner in which the persons are indwelling is according to sanctifying grace. Sanctifying grace is the effect that follows upon the invisible mission of a person, such that the creature is sanctified. While the notion of sanctifying grace has often been reified in Catholic theology, hinting that in justification the believer receives a form, with which he must cooperate for his justification, this need not be the case. Protestants rightly worry that such a notion of sanctifying grace in the process of justification entails a synergy that makes salvation partly a human affair. However, the reification of the notion of sanctifying grace is not necessary even for Aquinas. This sanctifying grace, which takes the shape of the supernatural virtues of faith and love, is not some reality independent of the divine persons which are thereby coming to the believer. Rather, sanctifying grace is precisely the formality by which the persons come to be assimilated in the believer. The gifts of knowledge and love, as sanctifying grace, are merely the created participations of the creature in the uncreated relations of the Trinity. They are the form that is consequent upon the invisible mission, in the same way that the seal is the consequent form, or the imprint in wax of the royal ring.

To stress, as Aquinas does, that these are *created* participations does not undermine the immediacy of the divine persons to the believer. It only clarifies the form such a presence takes, given that the persons are already present in virtue of their immensity. Roman Catholic theology has recently tended to follow Rahner in his attempt to reverse the priority of created versus uncreated grace, inherited from Augustine and Aquinas. As we have seen, this priority means that the manner in which a divine person is received is according to created grace. But this created grace, being an effect of the inseparable divine operations, does not appear to relate the believer specifically to the divine persons in their uniqueness, but only in an appropriated manner. Thus the gift of knowledge, whilst being created in us by the whole Trinity, is *appropriated* to the Son. The supernatural grace of knowledge, however, is not a specific operation of the Son himself. Neither is the supernatural grace of love a distinct work of the Spirit in us. These are the common works of the Trinity, shedding only the light of appropriation upon the distinct persons.

Rahner's Quasi-Formality Again

For Rahner and others, this prevents us from enjoying the distinct relations to the divine persons now as *wayfarers*, despite the fact that such relations will be enjoyed, as Aquinas himself admits, by the *comprehensors*, i.e., those enjoying the beatific vision. This introduces a dualism between the *life of grace* and the *life of glory*. In the present life, we receive created gifts, with which we cooperate, and therefore merit the life of glory. But this merit can be construed only in legal and moral terms, with no intrinsic connection between the two stages. Rahner suggests that our enjoyment of the triune persons in their distinctiveness and personal property in the life of glory is already anticipated by the invisible missions. That is, the indwelling of the Son and Spirit are not merely created gifts that are appropriated to these persons. Rather, we are given the persons themselves, such that "the life of glory is the definitive flowering (the 'manifestation,' the 'disclosure') of the life of divine sonship already possessed and merely 'hidden' for the moment."[5]

As we have already seen in chapter 1, Rahner suggests that such relations are to take place in terms of a quasi-formal causality of the divine persons. The persons invisibly indwelling us are transmitting the believer a share in their form. That is, they become the quasi-form of the believer's knowledge (Son) and love (Spirit). Without getting too deeply into the dungeons of this very technical philosophical discussion, we will note at least one problem: while in the case of the incarnation there might be an initial plausibility to the idea that the Son lends his existence to the human nature assumed, given the enhypostasia, to say this with regard to the indwelling persons risks turning the indwelling into another incarnation. The distinction between the two is essential and universally acknowledged, including by Rahner. In the indwelling, as opposed to the incarnation, it is human persons, that is, already actualized natures that are indwelt. To say that the Spirit becomes the (even quasi-) form of the believers' knowledge destroys the personal autonomy of our human nature. It means that what actualizes the nature (or certain operations of this nature) is not its personal, or hypostatic, center but the Holy Spirit. But this means that either this nature, or those operations, or both no longer belong to the human person that is indwelt. This is the equivalent of a pneumatological Apollinarism.

There are other significant objections to Rahner's proposal, but we will limit our critique. Let's try to illustrate the difficulties with this notion in the language of *Flatland*. When a sphere passes through Flatland, what appears in the experience of the Flatlanders is a circle. But what is this circle? It clearly does not have an autonomous existence in Flatland. The notion of a formal cause is an Aristotelian way of getting at what makes a thing to be the particular thing that it is. So, let's ask: what makes this particular thing, which phenomenologically is a circle, the particular thing that it is? It might seem that the obvious answer is: the sphere! Sure, the sphere's passing causes the *experience* of the circle for the Flatlanders. And yet a circle

---

5. Rahner, "Some Implications of the Scholastic Concept," 326.

is manifestly not a sphere, but only a section of a sphere. One might say that this circle forms a part of a sphere, but to say that a circle *is* a sphere is patently false.

This highlights the difficulty with applying the categories of formal causality to cross-dimensional causation: the distinctions between the two ontological orders are blurred. Strictly speaking, what makes this particular thing in the experience of the Flatlander a circle is *roundness*, or whatever we might call the essence of a circle. Or, take the example of Plato's cave dwellers. While the shadows projected on the cave wall are caused by people and fire, the shadows are neither people nor fire. That is, the formal cause of the shadows is neither humanity, nor people, nor fire.

These examples might have helped clarify what is at stake in the use of these notions. Rahner is certainly right in his intuition: he wants to tighten up the relationship that exists between the created effect of a mission (whether the human nature of Christ, or the infused knowledge and love in the invisible missions) and the person who is present in those created effects. But to say that the person is the (quasi-) formal cause of those effects confuses the two ontological dimensions. While the created effect is certainly caused by the mission (i.e., there would be no human nature of Christ were it not for the Son's mission, or no infused love were it not for the invisible mission of the Spirit), the created effect remains created, just as the manifest circle is a circle and not a sphere, and the Platonic shadows are just shadows, and not people or fire. Rahner is grasping after a conceptual way of stressing the unity between the mission and the created effect. Yet in the process he is risking blurring the distinction between immanence and transcendence.

We shall take up in the next section Rahner's important concern, that the invisible missions must reveal personal relations to the unique triune persons. It will help, however, to develop the idea that the respective formalities of the indwelling Son and Spirit are *knowledge* and *love*.

Knowledge and Love as the Form of the Invisible Missions

We have seen that both the visible and the invisible mission of the Son is productive of knowledge. The Son makes the Father known: "You have seen me; you have seen the Father!" The Son is the self-reflection of the Father, his spitting image, the perfect representation and mirroring of the Father. We know the Father by knowing the Son. But as long as the Son has only a visible mission, the knowledge it produces is liable to misinterpretation: "He came to his own, and his own people did not receive him" (John 1:11). The physical eyes and natural knowledge lack the ability to truly grasp the Logos. As Augustine explains, when the Logos is understood, we are no longer in this world. Unless the Son proceeds not only visibly but also invisibly, the objective data of his revelation may not be properly understood.

Without faith, the true significance of Jesus of Nazareth is only a bare history, open to a variety of interpretations, like any other historical event. Let us invoke the Flatland analogy again: how can any Flatlander ever know that he is faced not only with a circle but with a sphere, given that Flatlanders lack the capacity to experience a sphere? It is only when the sphere is (somehow supernaturally) lifting the Flatlander in the three-dimensional world that he is able to understand his own experience. In other words, a sphere may not be empirically experienced as a simple object, not unless the sphere itself elevates the Flatlander into its domain.

Faith, thus, is the gift whereby the true light of knowledge of Christ is received. In faith, Christ is truly received, truly experienced, precisely because faith is a supernatural gift. In faith, the human person is, like the Flatlander, elevated above his natural operations, to taste Christ, to share in him. Luther explained it well: the true content of faith is Christ; Christ is *forma fidei*, the form of faith. To have faith is to possess Christ.

In faith, the subject-object dualism anticipates its mending. Faith is not an inferior kind of knowledge or the antechamber of true knowledge. Faith, rather, is the attaining to the object of knowledge through the very operations of the thing known. In a certain sense, in every act of knowledge, there is a presence of the thing known in the knower. The formality of such a presence, now that we are familiar with this kind of conceptuality, is the conceptual and cognitive form present in the mind when something outside the mind is known. When I perceive the line of trees in front of my house, it is not the trees themselves that are present in my mind, as trees, but rather they are present in the form of images, concepts, and so on. My knowledge is mediated entirely by the concepts that lie within my operational capacity.

In faith, on the other hand, the object known becomes a subject! Paul senses this, and in one of his signal chapters on the invisible missions, chapter 4 of Galatians, he says that not only do we now know God but rather have become known by God (Gal 4:9). That is, we begin to know God through Godself. We know God through his own self-knowledge, that is, through Jesus Christ, the incarnate Word, the perfect representation of the Father (Col 1:15).

Gilles Emery explains this beautifully, with reference to Aquinas: in the invisible missions we do not have a merely natural knowledge, which does indeed have its utility, but rather these missions "enable us to reach 'right up to God himself' (*ad ipsum Deum*)."[6] God, he explains, is not just attained as a cause reflected in his effects (natural theology), "but touched upon in his own being, as the ultimate end pure and simple."[7]

For this reason, without the invisible missions there can be no true revelation of the divine persons. As an efficient cause, God acts inseparably, as one. Yet in the missions, we are given a taste of the very life of God himself. God is no longer just an external object of knowledge. As such an object, he may never be truly known in his deepest nature. Rather, through the presence of the persons, God is making himself the subject of our own knowledge. He assimilates into our knowledge and love, perfecting these with himself and yet preserving their integrity.

This faith, whose form is Christ, yielding as it does true knowledge, necessarily leads to true love. Love, which is the created participation in the Holy Spirit (yet to be explained), is ordered to knowledge. If in knowledge the object known comes to exist in a certain manner in the knower, in love, the object loved also comes to exist in a certain form in the lover. One is the realization of the other's presence in our mind, the other in our wills. Emery again puts it well: "When we have an intellectual presence, the known reality is present through its likeness; whereas, in the will, the beloved entity is present through a dynamic momentum, as attracting us toward itself."[8] This dynamic movement is love itself. Aquinas summarizes these formalities succinctly: "God dwells in human beings through the faith which operates by charity."[9]

Eleonore Stump: Mutual Within-ness

Eleonore Stump has recently made a very intriguing suggestion about the modality of the indwelling persons. She defines indwelling as "mutual

---

6. Emery, *Trinitarian Theology*, 382.
7. Emery, *Trinitarian Theology*, 382.
8. Emery, *Trinitarian Theology*, 381.
9. Aquinas, *In 1 Cor.*, 3:16 (no. 172), quoted in Emery, *Trinitarian Theology*, 384n112.

within-ness of individual psyches or persons"[10] and she appeals to the phenomenon of shared attention as an explanatory framework. In shared attention, she observes, there is a mirroring of the thoughts and sensations of one person in another. Thus,

> when Paula empathizes with Jerome in his pain, Paula has a painful feeling; and the painful feeling that she has is her feeling; and she feels and understands it as Jerome's feeling of pain. By rough analogy, in union *simpliciter* between Paula and Jerome, Paula has Jerome's psyche somehow accessible *within her own*; only she feels and understands that accessible psyche as Jerome's, not hers.[11]

We have often had that experience. When you see someone hurt a foot, receive an injection, have a toothache, it is as if you would have these experiences, only you are not perceiving them as yours but as this other person's. Neuroscientists explain that there is an activation in the phenomenon of shared attention of so-called mirror neurons. The very same neurons that are activated when Jerome has the pain are also activated when Paula sees Jerome being in pain.

This model has particular explanatory power for Stump. Because God has become a human being, he not only knows the human beings as their Creator and Sustainer, but these humans are also present in some sense in himself by virtue of this shared attention. Christ also internalizes human sin, through this same process. Stump observes that when we see people doing evil things, in virtue of the same mechanism, our conscience becomes in a certain sense soiled by what we have seen. In this way we may understand Christ's having become sin (2 Cor 5:21). Moreover, in virtue of the same mechanism of shared attention, divine persons can become present to human beings. To have the Holy Spirit, then, is to have a mutual closeness with him, in such a way that his thoughts and his emotional states become your very own emotional states.

This explanation of the indwelling of the Holy Spirit in terms of mutual closeness is certainly helpful. Stump appears to preserve the necessary mediation of a receiving form for the Holy Spirit. The Spirit is not present as himself, but through the formality of certain affections of the will, or what she calls "the offices of love."[12]

---

10. Stump, *Atonement*, 117.
11. Stump, *Atonement*, 117.
12. Stump, *Atonement*, 123.

In our view, what is missing from Stump's otherwise impressive account is the manner in which this love, which is the form of the Spirit's indwelling, is not simply the believer's love in general but particularly Christ's love of the Father. This is where the theology of missions makes an important contribution to this discussion. As we have seen, the external procession of the Spirit comes by way of the human nature of Jesus Christ. The Spirit is shaped for us, formed for us by Christ himself. This can be taken as a friendly Protestant amendment to the Catholic view that the inhabitation takes place by created grace. This created grace, in this case, love, is not simply a habit in the believer but precisely the love that gradually grew in Christ as he was perfected in obedience and in the face of suffering.

Christ's Own Love

This is another manner in which the love which is the Spirit in us is ordered to the faith, which is the presence of our Lord. We receive the Holy Spirit by placing our faith in Christ and by arriving at mutual closeness precisely with Christ. Love is poured into our hearts (Rom 5:5) precisely because of our clinging to Christ in faith. In the personal encounter with the living Christ, his love stings us in our complacency. The demonstration of this love takes place supremely on the cross. There is here a truth to the moral example/influence theory of the atonement, particularly as expressed by Peter Abelard. Christ's love has a magnetic power, a force that draws us to him. This is the loveliness of Christ, viz., the perfect quality of his love, which mysteriously moves our wills as well. Christ is thus the perfect human being in which these missions are realized, and our receiving these missions is conditioned upon our being in him. Thus, the love we have for God is not simply a human love but the very theandric love of Christ, to which some are irresistibly drawn, just as our thoughts and mind are now the mind of Christ (Phil 2:5): "It is no longer I who live, but Christ who lives in me" (Gal 2:20). Just as the first needle attached to the magnet can pass on this magnetism to other needles clinging to it, so Christ's love is necessarily poured into the hearts of those who cling to him by faith. For this reason, John makes so much of love as the evidence of belonging to Christ.

This approach through the missions, and in particular through the idea of a love formed by Christ, can potentially move the ecumenical needle, so to speak, and draw Protestants and Catholics closer. The Catholic insistence that faith must be formed by love (*fides caritas formata*) is not welcomed by

Protestants, who fear synergy, as this love is precisely the habitual love of the believer. But if we understand that the love that forms faith is not our habitual love but precisely Christ's contagious love, Protestants, too, can accept this broader definition of faith as formed by love. Faith, then, cannot be a mere operation of the believer. It is a drawing into the Trinity by the indwelling Son, a self-communication of the Son to the believer. For that reason, because it is a mission, it cannot fail to be accompanied by the love poured by the Spirit in his own mission. The two inward missions are not separable. Counterfeit faith is precisely faith as a human work, a human operation. It is not a faith instrumentalized by the indwelling of the Son, and therefore not leading to love.

One question remains to be clarified in regards to the invisible missions. How can faith and love be the created forms by which we receive the divine persons, when, as created, they are effects of the common divine causality? Can Rahner's concerns be addressed such that we affirm the reality of distinct relations to the triune persons and not simply appropriated ones? It will be argued in this next and final section of the chapter that the finality of the missions is a real enjoyment of the distinct persons of the Trinity.

THE FINALITY OF THE INVISIBLE MISSIONS

Several clarifications must be made as a preparation for our answer to Rahner's concerns. Rahner's reasonable desire is to illuminate the manner in which the divine missions relate us to the triune persons in their *propria*. In order to explain how, perhaps despite appearances, this is still the case, we need to clarify what a divine person is. We shall explain how the Latin account of the divine persons makes possible such distinct relations to the divine persons.

Triune Personhood

The problem of triune personhood is notoriously complex. Our account falls squarely within a Latin approach to this problem, where the persons are defined as *subsistent relations*. A puzzling notion for many, the idea of a subsistent relation is analogous to the relations within a magnet between the two poles. It may be said that each of the poles is a function of a relationality that characterizes the magnet as a whole, which might be called the magnetic field. Within this magnetic field an irreducible *taxis* may be observed, from North to South. Moreover, these poles and the magnetic relation are mutually constitutive, such that you do not have one without the other. Neither are the poles parts of the magnet, such that removing one would leave the magnet or the pole itself intact.

This analogy illuminates to a certain extent the nature of the persons in the Latin tradition. Father, Son, and Holy Spirit are functions of the various relations that exist within the divine essence and that are in fact mutually constitutive with the essence. In the Latin tradition, starting with Augustine, and building in particular on John's theology of the Word, these relations are defined in terms of the substantial activities of the divine essence, intellect and will. In the essential activity of intellect, by which God knows himself, the internal and eternal Word is proceeding. Conversely, in the essential activity of will, we have Love proceeding. As Aquinas explains: "That which knows itself and loves itself is in itself, not only by a real identity, but also in the capacity of the known in the knower, and the beloved in the lover."[13] The real identity implies the divine unity, while the presence of the known in the knower indicates a relational distinction.

Since the persons are equiprimordial with the essence, and not its functions (modalism), or by themselves constituting the essence (as in social trinitarianism), the persons are impossible to define without the essence. As John Owen put it, they are the divine essence, under a relational property. Thus, when we are asking about distinct relations with the divine persons, it must be remembered that the persons are only given together with the essence, and thus together with each other. We may consider the analogy of the wine taster: the various aromas and nuances of the wine cannot be tasted separately from one another. The sensing organs are affected by the whole wine. And yet the expert taster is able to isolate these distinct notes, not because he tastes them individually, but rather because he recognizes a note in inseparable unity with the other notes.

A Tasting of the Persons' Personal Properties

The analogy of the wine tasting is not accidental, since the invisible missions of the divine persons entail a certain "tasting" of the Trinity. The reason the persons are identified is because the persons are transmitting to us a certain participation in their personal identity. Just as in wine tasting there is a

13. Aquinas, *ST* I, q. 37, art. 1.

certain communication of the various components of the wine, through the olfactory and salivary glands, so in the indwelling of the divine persons there is a created participation in the uncreated relations which define the persons. Thus, the faith and hope that we receive as supernatural virtues are created participations in the uncreated intellectual and volitional relations whereby Love and Word proceed.

Such a transformation of the person indwelt is according to his own operations of intellect and volition. The missions thus indicate a fruition of the persons outside of the divine essence. The divine self-knowledge is shared with human beings, through the mission of the Word, such that God is not only known by the creatures but also resembled by them. Similarly, the divine self-love is poured into the creatures by the Holy Spirit, which has been given to them, such that God is present in them as the beloved is present in the lover.

The persons thus are related to the believer distinctly in the sense that the believer receives a distinct sharing in their personal property. The persons leave an imprint upon the believer, in knowledge and in love. While the imprint is *created*, it nevertheless leads to the enjoyment of the divine person. Emery explains the connection between the gift of created grace and the uncreated persons in this way: "The gifts of grace, that is, of wisdom and charity, are a *disposition* to receiving the divine person, and it is because of this that the weight is on the human side of the event. Created gifts of grace are necessary in order to 'proportion' a human being to the divine persons, that is, in order to raise the human soul so as to make it capable of attaining God, or of being divinized."[14] The disposition of the human being must not be understood as a moment temporally prior to the indwelling of the person. Using the conceptuality of the missions, it can be said that this disposing of the creature is only a consequent condition of the mission, and not something which makes the mission itself possible.

By the gifts of grace, we are enabled to recognize the person of the Son and the Spirit. The persons thus become manifest for us, like the wine notes become manifest for the taster. This is a truly *experiential knowledge*. It is not discursive knowledge, for in such knowledge, the dualism of subject and object is still strong. In the experiential knowledge given in the invisible missions, we are given a *foretaste* of the final union between subject and object, between the knower and the known. This is the kind of knowledge in which we are known, a knowledge turned on its head by the object who

---

14. Emery, *Trinitarian Theology*, 385.

becomes internal to us and thus subject. It is as if God is drawing us into his own self-knowledge, by sharing his Word with us. In the invisible mission, this Word is no longer external, a historical object, but internal, a Word of the heart, opening our eyes to himself.

Thus, in the invisible missions we really are in touch with the *propria* of the persons. The reason for this is not, *pace* Rahner, because we receive a quasi-formal communication of their existence. Rather, it is because we receive a created participation in the personal properties of the Son and Spirit: we are thus formed according to knowledge and love. The persons of the Son and Spirit do not become the (quasi-) form of our intellect and love. Such would annul the autonomy and freedom of these faculties. No, our intellect and love are already formed according to the personal actualization of our human nature. Instead, our intellect and our volition receive the supernatural gifts that dispose them to enjoy the persons, by receiving and being shaped according to the personal properties of the persons.

Divine Persons as Exemplars

In the categories of causality, Aquinas expresses this in terms of *exemplary causality*. In the invisible missions, the persons become the exemplar causes. This is to say that the creature is shaped according to the personal properties of the Son and Spirit, Word and Love. Aquinas explains that the "proper relation belonging to the divine person is represented in the soul through a sort of received likeness, whose exemplar and origin is the property of this same eternal relation."[15]

The finality of the invisible missions is indeed the divine persons considered in their propria. But their propria do not consist in distinct individual properties but exclusively in the relations that they comport within the unity of the divine essence. Thus, the Son bears the relation property of being begotten as Image, while the Spirit bears the relation property of proceeding as Love from the Father and Son. The missions do take us all the way to the persons, but it may not be in the way we might have anticipated. The persons make themselves manifest precisely in the distinct imprints they leave upon our beings. We do not therefore *recognize* the persons in a detached, objectifying kind of way. Rather, we recognize them in our very depths, as the Image is fashioned in us and as Love is kindled.

---

15. Aquinas, *In Sent*, dist. 15, q. 4, art. 1, as translated by Emery, *Trinitarian Theology*, 376.

The more we grow in our knowledge and love, the more shall we know the Son and the Spirit. The invisible missions work to enlarge our capacity for God. Our desire for God grows the more our knowledge and love grow. Our taste for the three persons becomes more refined, the more we enjoy them. C. S. Lewis has put it beautifully: "The instrument through which you see God is your whole self. And if a man's self is not kept clean and bright, his glimpse of God will be blurred."[16] This transformation is still imperfect though, as long as we are *in via*. Only in the beatific vision will this be completed, but in what sense? If we already have the persons as our truest end, if they have already given themselves through their gifts, of what consists the beatific vision? We shall leave that question for the final chapter of our discussion, after we have probed some implications of the invisible missions in ecclesiology and missiology.

MISSIO DEI AND THE ORDER OF THE MISSIONS

The concept of *missio Dei* has been one of the organizing motifs of missiology since the second half of the twentieth century. Its fundamental thesis is that mission is primarily an activity of God and not of the church. The new framework has proven itself to be of quite an enduring value. However, the scaffolding upon which it is erected surprisingly fails to draw on the theology of the divine missions. The question naturally arises about the contribution of our theology of the divine missions to the current conversation about *missio Dei*.

Developments in Missiology

The first missiologist to introduce the notion was Karl Hartenstein, in 1952, as David Bosch reports.[17] The appeal of the concept was its ability to orient missions in a post-colonial setting, where the idea that the church might be God's missionary agency became increasingly offensive to a budding post-colonial sensitivity. The mission of the church follows the mission of God in the world. But this assumes that there is a mission of God that is already present and distinct from the mission of the church. As Aagaard

---

16. Lewis, *Mere Christianity*, 141.

17. We draw this historical report about the concept of *missio Dei* from David Bosch's *Transforming Mission*, 401.

notes, "There is church because there is mission, not vice versa."[18] Or, as another important motive force behind the shift, Jürgen Moltmann, puts it, "It is not the church that has a mission of salvation to fulfill in the world; it is the mission of the Father through the Son and the Spirit that includes the church."[19]

One does not have to wait very long for the worrying consequences of this shift to sink in. If there is a mission of God outside of the church, in which the latter also participates, and considering the fact that the church is, after all, the body of Christ (and the temple of the Holy Spirit), it appears that there are independent divine missions. Assuming, with most *missio Dei* proponents, that the mission of God outside of the church is carried out by the Holy Spirit, the rift between the mission of the Spirit and that of the Son seemed inevitable. The discussion drifted away from the intentions of Hartenstein and others, such that many missiologists expressed serious misgivings about it. Rosin called the concept a "Trojan horse."[20] Bosch summarizes the conflict: "Those who supported the wider understanding of the concept tended to radicalize the view that the Missio Dei was larger than the mission of the church, even to the point of suggesting that it excluded the church's involvement."[21] A report by the World Council of Churches study committee on the missionary structure of the congregation even went as far as to say, "The church serves the *missio Dei* in the world... [when] it points to God at work in world history and names him there."[22]

For many involved in the missiological conferences such as the Uppsala Assembly (1967), the mission of God was described in terms of *shalom* or, alternatively, as humanization. Starting from the idea that "it is the world that must be allowed to provide the agenda for the churches,"[23] conversion was reduced to social change.

Although the earlier conversations about the *missio Dei* often seemed to gravitate towards an understanding of the work of God in terms of social justice, or what today is fashionably called "human flourishing," the role of other religions in this divine mission was also gradually brought to the fore.

---

18. Aagaard, "Missio Dei in katolischer Sicht," 423.
19. Moltmann, *Church in the Power*, 64.
20. Rosin, *Missio Dei*, 26.
21. Bosch, *Transforming Mission*, 293.
22. Bosch, *Transforming Mission*, 293.
23. World Council of Churches, *Church for Others*, 20.

Roman Catholic Theology of Religions

In Roman Catholic theology there has been an increased tendency to speak of other religions as bearers of a universal gift of the Spirit. This trajectory culminates in Pope Francis claiming that "the pluralism and the diversity of *religions*, colour, sex, race and language are willed by God in His wisdom, through which He created human beings."[24]

Some of the earliest seeds of this were planted by the theology of Karl Rahner, whose concept of "anonymous Christians" opens the way for regarding other faiths as bearers of salvation in some sense. In "Jesus Christ in the Non-Christian Religions," Rahner claims that "Christ is present and efficacious in the non-Christian believer (and therefore in the non-Christian religions) through his Spirit."[25] Rahner's work was taken a step further in Peter Phan's *Being Religious Interreligiously: Asian Perspectives on Interfaith Dialogue*.[26] Phan makes a number of contentious claims, such as the Spirit "operates salvifically beyond the Logos" and "God's saving presence through God's Word and Spirit is not limited to Judeo-Christian history but is extended to the whole of human history and may be seen especially in the sacred books, rituals, moral teachings, and spiritual practices of all religions."[27]

Evangelical Contribution: Amos Yong

Perhaps the most significant evangelical contribution to such a development can be found in the work of Amos Yong. Although not drawing explicitly on the notion of *missio Dei*, Yong's *Beyond the Impasse: Toward a Pneumatological Theology of Religions* defends the same fundamental idea, viz., that there is a presence and work of the Spirit, mediating salvation in some sense, in other religions. He asserts that "the religions of the world, like everything else that exists, are providentially sustained by the Spirit of God for divine purposes."[28] The Spirit of God has been "poured out upon all people" (Acts 2:17), which Yong insists should be taken literally to refer to a universal pouring out of the Spirit over all humanity.

---

24. Francis, "Document on Human Fraternity," para. 27.
25. Rahner, "Jesus Christ in Non-Christian Religions," 43.
26. See Phan, *Being Religious Interreligiously*.
27. Phan, *Being Religious Interreligiously*, 65.
28. Yong, *Beyond the Impasse*, 46.

Yong certainly is right to affirm a presence of the Spirit in other religions in the sense that God underlies every culture, all that exists, by his omnipresence. But Yong appears to claim much more than just such a presence, even though he will not commit on the question of salvation in other faiths. The presence of the Spirit is the kind of presence that requires discernment; thus it is clear that this does not refer to presence by immensity as we have defined it. The Spirit is already at work in other religions, whether or not this work is in itself salvific, independently of a confession of Christ.

What may be observed in the writers above is an enlargement of the mission of God beyond the boundaries and activity of the church. We now have to ask how this kind of theology is consistent with an orthodox articulation of the missions of the Son and the Spirit. While the formulation of the idea of *missio Dei* usually lacks such a discussion, important contributions have been made by Karl Rahner, Frederick Crowe, and Amos Yong. The fundamental argument of these writers is that the mission of the Spirit precedes the mission of the Son.

Rahner: Spirit as Entelechy

Rahner is aware that a difficulty with his proposal is the New Testament description of the Spirit as the Spirit of Christ. We have also noted the danger that a non-ecclesial conception of grace appears to ascribe an economy to the Holy Spirit that is autonomous from the Son's mission. His solution is innovative and not without some merit. "This Spirit is always, everywhere, and from the outset the entelechy, the determining principle, of the history of revelation and salvation; and its communication and acceptance, by its very nature, never takes place in a merely abstract, transcendental form."[29] Or, "the universal efficacy of the Spirit is directed from the very beginning to the zenith of its historical mediation, which is the Christ event."[30] We can thus think of the Son as the final cause[31] of the sending of the Spirit, as opposed to its efficient cause. In this way is the Spirit the Spirit of Christ, not because Christ in some way makes possible or enables the sending of the Spirit.

---

29. Rahner, "Jesus Christ in Non-Christian Religions," 46.
30. Rahner, "Jesus Christ in Non-Christian Religions," 46.
31. Rahner, "Jesus Christ in Non-Christian Religions," 46.

The opposite suggestion is then made, that of seeing the Spirit as the cause of the incarnation and of atonement. Eschewing a "Christology from above," Rahner argues that the incarnation can be understood as an emergence from within humanity's openness to transcendence, under the influence of the Spirit. This leads Rahner to a different understanding of saving faith as "the seeking *memoria* of the absolute bringer of salvation,"[32] something compatible with other savior figures. The Spirit is the *entelechy* of history, the motive force driving it towards Jesus Christ. Rahner is convinced that he is still able to affirm the bond between the Spirit and Christ, in the sense that the Spirit ultimately leads to Christ.

Crowe: Love before Knowledge

The work of Frederick E. Crowe self-consciously carries over the legacy of Bernard Lonergan, a towering figure in trinitarian theology. Crowe has argued that the two missions have traditionally been cast in the wrong order. Even though in the visible order it is the Son who is first manifested, this must not be taken at its face value. He offers the following thesis: "We have simply to reverse the order in which commonly we think of the Son and Spirit in the world. Commonly we think of God first sending the Son, and of the Spirit being sent in that context, to bring to completion the work of the Son. The thesis says that, on the contrary, God first sent the Spirit, and then sent the Son in the context of the Spirit's mission, to bring to completion—perhaps not precisely the work of the Spirit, but the work which God conceived as one work to be executed in the two steps of the twofold mission of first the Spirit and then the Son."[33]

Crowe also provides two very insightful analogies for this. The first thing we receive from our parents is love, he argues. Only then and because of that do we receive food and other necessities, such as education, safety, a home, etc. In good Thomistic fashion, love stands in for the Holy Spirit. It is love that stands at the foundation of every other activity. Similarly, it is the Holy Spirit that stands at the foundation of explicit faith.

Crowe supplies a similar analogy from Lonergan. Before two lovers ever get to the point of confessing their love and feelings for one another, there is a period where they each can be said to be "in love" with one another. The mutual confession of their common love, their making this love

---

32. Rahner, "Jesus Christ in Non-Christian Religions," 46.
33. Crowe, "Son of God," 325.

explicit, is not an entirely new habit of love but a confirmation and consolidation of what had been there before. Similarly, Crowe explains, God has poured his love into the world, and the world does indeed respond in a sort of love even before this love is made explicit in the sending of his Son (John 3:16). Crowe meditates on this most intriguing fact, that "God does not declare this love from the beginning."[34] "There is the prolonged silence of the ages when God loves secretly, when the Spirit is present in us incognito, when in an almost human manner God holds back from a declaration of Love. Then at last, in this the final age, and in the most eloquent manner possible, the avowal is made; God's love is declared, and the one and only Son is sent to be our savior."[35]

It may thus be said that the Spirit of God is already at work in the world before Christ, and indeed besides Christ, wherever human persons are moved towards God. Putting his own twist on Rahner's idea of "anonymous Christians," Crowe suggests we call other religious believers "Spiritans,"[36] since "they have their own spiritual priesthood exercised in the interior temple of the Spirit."[37] Christians and adherents of other faiths share a "common gifting with the Spirit."[38]

Yong: A Pneumatology of Other Religions

Like Rahner and Crowe, Yong also seeks to ground a pneumatological theory of religions in the primacy of the Spirit's mission. By foregrounding the mission of the Spirit, the dualism between christological particularity and the cosmic Christ can be resolved. He appeals to *Spirit Christology* to identify the Spirit himself in Christ: "Jesus the Christ is both the incarnate logos (or concrete form) and the anointed pneuma (inner dynamic field of force)."[39] We cannot expand on these complex and very insightful notions developed by Yong in this connection. He draws on the ancient Irenaean tradition of the Son and Spirit as the two hands of God at work in creation. Every phenomenon exhibits the twofold dimensions of concrete form, which he ascribes to the Son/Logos, and an inner dynamic field of force,

---

34. Crowe, "Son of God," 330.
35. Crowe, "Son of God," 330.
36. Crowe, "Son of God," 335.
37. Crowe, "Son of God," 336.
38. Crowe, "Son of God," 335.
39. Yong, *Beyond the Impasse*, 135.

which pertains to the Spirit. Only by the movement of the Spirit is Christ recognizable as God; apart from him, he would be a mere human being. Conversely, in the world religions, we may also distinguish between their concrete form, which does not explicitly relate to Christ, and their own inner dynamic movement, where an anticipation and even longing for Christ could be discerned.

What about Paul's and John's statements that no one can confess Jesus as Lord except by the Holy Spirit (1 Cor 12:3) and that every spirit that does not confess Jesus is not from God (1 John 4:2–3)? Yong explains that "while discerning the Spirit is intimately connected with the Christ, this should not be understood in a way that subordinates the Spirit to Christ—as in, 'Ah, here is a confession of Jesus as Lord, and therefore we can be certain of the presence and activity of the Spirit!' in a simplistic sense—or that renders the Spirit subservient to the Word. Rather, Word and Spirit are mutually defining as the 'two hands of the Father.' This should alert us to the processive, ambiguous, and dialectical nature of discernment."[40]

The Logical Priority of the Son's Mission

All the three theologians above represent a growing movement in theology to reverse the order of the two missions, such that the Spirit's mission is constitutive of the incarnate personhood of Christ. Such a reversed order of the missions can buttress the shift in missiology towards a broader conception of the *missio Dei*. It can be shown, however, that the reversal of the order of the two missions is fundamentally misguided, and therefore it cannot be invoked in support of the broader conception of *missio Dei*. Moreover, a positive approach to the work of the Spirit in other religions is possible from within a traditional ordering of the two missions.

In the account of missions we have been unpacking, which stresses that a mission indicates a union between a divine person and a created effect, it is impossible to predicate that the mission of the Spirit comes before the mission of the Son. The fundamental difference between the mission of the Son and that of the Spirit is that in the former the created effect is brought into existence in the very act of the hypostatic union. The created effect indicated by the Spirit's mission, on the other hand, already exists. This is the fundamental difference between the Son's mission by hypostatic union and the Spirit's mission. Therefore, if the Spirit's mission would

40. Yong, *Beyond the Impasse*, 169.

precede the Son's, it would mean that a created effect must already exist before the hypostatic union. This Nestorian option was decisively rejected in the Chalcedonian controversies. One could say that the created effect does not preexist the Spirit's mission but is itself created at the moment of the mission itself; but in this case one would speak of an incarnation of the Spirit himself, since such an effect is brought into existence by the mission of the Spirit himself. However, everything about the human nature of Christ belongs to the Son by virtue of the hypostatic union. There is no substance in Christ that is in hypostatic union with the Spirit. The fundamental Christian doctrine of the incarnation of the Son alone fundamentally stands in the way of this affirmation of a mission of the Spirit prior to the Son's.

This reveals the fundamental vulnerability of much Spirit Christology: it confuses the unique act of the incarnation with other missions by which the divine persons unite themselves with created substances for the purpose of sanctification. The tradition we have been expounding clarifies that whatever activities of the Spirit (and the Son) are to be encountered prior to Christ are not missions but operations. We have elaborated this distinction at some length in this volume. Similarly, the contribution of the Spirit in the conception of Christ is not, strictly speaking, a mission but an operation. As an operation, it is only *appropriated* to the Spirit, since all divine persons indivisibly participate in it.

The Spirit's sanctification of Christ is accomplished not from a position of hypostatic union with the divine nature. Only the Son is hypostatically united to a human nature, and therefore, as Stăniloae and Lossky point out, the Spirit does not give himself to us hypostatically, but only in the hypostasis of the Son himself.[41]

As Yong himself realizes, even Eastern Orthodoxy, with its strong pneumatology, appears to subordinate the Spirit to Christ. We found this to be fitting with both the witness of the New Testament (the Spirit of Christ), and with the procession of the Spirit *filioque*. While the Orthodox reject the procession of the Spirit from the Son as well, they nevertheless insist that the Spirit proceeds in order to rest upon the Son. But very few theologians have ventured as far as to suggest that the Son proceeds by way of the Spirit (*spirituque*).

---

41. Stăniloae, "Procession of the Holy Spirit"; Lossky, *Mystical Theology*, 159.

Thus, in claiming that the Spirit proceeds externally before the Son, theologians like Crowe and Yong,[42] besides flattening out the uniqueness of the incarnation by comparison to other missions, also downplay the fact that the Spirit is manifested hypostatically precisely by Christ, or at least in connection to Christ. They further minimize the importance of what we have called the *Christoformation* of the Spirit, tied to the fact that only upon Christ's ascension can the Spirit of Christ be sent. The biblical description of the Spirit's mission clearly orders it to the Son's mission.

The uniqueness of Christianity, we again have to insist, is not that it contains a unique *activity* of the Spirit or of the Son. Rather, it consists in the profession of an ontological *union* with the divine persons, signified by the language of the *indwelling*. In sanctifying grace, we are formally united with the Spirit himself. Thus, grace is not just any created effect but precisely a created effect that is a consequent of the mission of the Spirit. The church's uniqueness consists, in other words, precisely in its participation in a supernatural order, in the very life of the Trinity, and not in some further created blessing. For this reason, the finality of the invisible missions is precisely the enjoyment of the divine persons in their hypostatic character. In these supernatural relations, we are tasting of the eternal self-knowledge and self-love of God, anticipating and preparing for the perfection of the beatific vision.

It is perhaps not surprising that such recent shifts in missiology, which tend to conflate divine missions and activities, also tend to deflate the supernatural dimension of the church's life, by comparison with the operation of grace in other religions. This obscures the fact that although there may be a divine activity in other religions, this activity is qualitatively different from a divine mission. For this reason, to speak of a "gift" of the Spirit outside of the body of Christ can be done only by flattening out the true supernatural nature of the Spirit's gift. Such a gift can be received only in conjunction with Christ, since the participation in the procession of the Spirit can only take place downstream from our baptism into the Son's procession.

The Spirit's Work in Other Religions

Now, we have claimed that it is possible to give a positive account of the work of God in other religions from this perspective as well. We can only

---

42. Rahner hesitates to make this move in the doctrine of the missions. David Coffey thinks there is an inconsistency here. See his "'Incarnation' of the Holy Spirit."

indicate the contours of such an account here, acknowledging at the same time that the issues are very complex. In this Western tradition, the formality of the Son's indwelling is knowledge, and of the Spirit's, love. Love is ordered to knowledge, for to love assumes at least some incipient knowledge. Yong quite helpfully affirms that there is a longing for God in other religions and in all world cultures. Rahner frames this in the language of a *searching memory* for God. On this basis, Yong concludes that there is already present a gift of the Spirit in the world.

We can readily admit that there is such a longing for God, perhaps even a desire for God, or a nostalgia for him, as John Paul II called it.[43] But at the same time it must be admitted that there is also some incipient knowledge of God in the world. So, by the same logic, it would have to be admitted that the Son was also sent as a gift in the world. Yet Yong does not make this move. He neatly assigns to the Spirit the work of drawing universal humanity towards God, and to the Son the work of particular historic manifestation.

Let us return for a moment to the logic of the missions. We have seen that the person sent into the world did not arrive at a new place. The doctrine of the missions recognizes that there was already a presence of the Son and Spirit in the world prior to their missions. So the claim that the Spirit is present and operative, inclusive of other religions, is in fact not a contested or problematic claim. But, crucially, it is balanced by the claim that the Son and the Father as well are present and active in all aspects of created reality, by virtue of their immensity. Christians can affirm that there is some knowledge of God but also some inchoate desire for God in humanity, and that this knowledge and desire is, as Paul puts it, ignorantly expressed in various forms of religious and cultural expression (cf. Acts 17:23, "what therefore you worship as unknown"). The same Paul acknowledges that some things are known about God even by those who do not believe, such that everyone is without excuse and responsible for this knowledge. But this knowledge is like that of a blind man, feeling his way around objects in complete darkness. Further, humanity's desire for God is often a love of self, or what it regards as good within it, while its utter self-transcendence reveals that its object really is God. Nevertheless, compared to actual love based on knowledge, it is more like melancholy and, indeed, nostalgia. It can be admitted that this partial knowledge and longing are expressed in

---

43. John Paul II, "Message of the Holy Father."

various religious and cultural forms. But these remain a dark and ignorant knowledge and a confused love.

Here we see the fundamental difference of Christianity. If being a Christian means having tasted and seen that God is good, since the divine self-knowledge and self-love are now internal, then this knowledge and love of God are qualitatively different from whatever knowledge and love of God are present outside the body of Christ. The object of Christian knowledge is not simply theoretical and discursive but internal and therefore experiential. The subject-object dualism, which represents the problem of knowledge, is mended or in the process of being overcome through the union of the believer with the Logos. Similarly, the love we have for the Father is not simply an imitation, a learned behavior, some sweet stirring, but supernaturally the very love that binds the Father and the Son, the Spirit himself. Surely now we have only a foretaste of the future banquet, but it is nevertheless a true tasting.

A Christian theology of religions must never relinquish the consciousness of this supernatural knowledge and love that we enjoy. The world's diverse religions can still be appreciated and valued as the bending of human activity and affections by the drawing power of God. The inner dynamism of other religions may indeed be taken to pull in the direction of God, and yet their natural inertia prevents them from finally giving in and finding their rest in union with God. We may again find the magnetic analogy helpful: God draws the whole world, like a magnet draws a needle, to himself. The drawing is done by the whole of the Godhead, not simply by the Spirit. As we have seen, the Son as well as the Spirit is present and active in the world. Yet until the needle is finally attached to the magnet, it will not receive its properties, even though it experiences its pull. The world's religions surely contain many demonstrations that human persons are conscious of a pull, of a longing and desire for some transcendent reality. But until we are united to the Logos, this longing is a groping in the dark.

The Exclusivity of Christ

The Scriptures instruct us that our landing in the triune life is precisely at the point of the Son. Just as a needle unites to a specific pole of the magnet, the person in grace is included in the Son. Since God is simple, it is not just the Son that the believer experiences and enjoys but the other persons as well. The Christian enjoys the Father, as the one revealed by the Son; and she enjoys the Spirit, as the one who comes from the Father *via* the Son. There is no other entry into the supernatural communion with the Trinity, except at the point of the Son. Christ is the sheep's gate; he is the way, the truth, and the life (John 14:6). As we have seen, the Holy Spirit comes to us from the humanity of Christ. Thus, sharing in Christ, and specifically sharing in the humanity of Christ, which includes having communion with his body and blood, represents the manner of receiving the gift of the Spirit.

Christ speaks of his Spirit as a river of living water, which flows from those who believe in him (John 7:37–39). The Spirit, then, flows not only from the side of Christ (*e latere Christi*) on the cross but from believers as well! This is precisely the supernatural character of the church as the body of Christ, which is not to be understood in merely natural or institutional terms but supernaturally and sacramentally. Just as Christ is the sheep's gate, so his ecclesial body is the conduit of the Spirit's indwelling in the world. This admits of operations and activities of the Spirit in the world, *extra ecclesiam*. But it denies that the Spirit proceeds to indwell others except through some form of mediation of the body of Christ.[44] While to some this may seem like the Spirit has been subordinated to Christ (indeed, even to the church!), it must be stressed that the Spirit is ordered only to the Son, just as the Son is ordered to the Father.

In conclusion, it can be seen how attention to the notion of a divine mission, dogmatically defined as a union between a procession and a created effect, resists the reversal of the traditional ordering of the two missions and the shift in missiology to a broader conception of the *missio Dei*. The church remains the privileged conduit, not of the divine operation and action in the world, where indeed natural ends may be accomplished through common grace in whichever religious and cultural province. Rather, it is the conduit of the supernatural divine self-communication, the indwelling of the Trinity in the souls of the justified. As for the supernatural end of participation in the life of the Trinity, it is reserved, on this side of eternity,[45]

---

44. This can be construed in many ways, and there is room for dispute here. For example, Miroslav Volf's ecclesiology accepts the ecclesial mediation of the faith of conversion, through the proclamation of the gospel by Christians. Catholics and Orthodox believers construe this ecclesial mediation necessarily in sacramental terms.

45. We have left unresolved the question of the eschatological salvation of those who have never heard the gospel. This discussion concerned exclusively the question of a supernatural participation in the Spirit outside the concrete body of Christ.

to those who are confessing Christ (1 John 4:15; Rom 10:9) and for whom his flesh is true food and his blood true drink (John 6:55–59).[46]

CONCLUSION

In the invisible missions of the Son and the Spirit we have the most precious gift of salvation. Much more than the removal of guilt, the gift consists in a participation in the very life of the Trinity, through the indwelling in the believer of the Father, Son, and Holy Spirit. We have analyzed in turn the reality, the formality, and the finality of the divine missions. We then applied our conclusions to an important conversation in contemporary missiology. Our project is driven by a concern about the domestication of the supernatural mystery of the gospel. On the theological right, there can be a reduction of the gospel to a judicial absolution; on the left, a leveling of the supremacy and exclusivity of Christianity and of the centrality of Christ. Both angles betray a sort of *ontological deflationism*, a reduction of the supernatural to the natural.

The indwelling of the divine persons, however, cannot be reduced to its forensic dimension, even though it necessarily presupposes it. Neither can it be reduced to moral transformation. Additionally, the beloved categories of human flourishing, of *shalom*, etc., are but the shadow of the ultimate drama, which is that of the elevation of human beings into the very life of God, at the point of the Son.

In the invisible missions we are given a foretaste of eternity, but a real taste nevertheless. In the experiential knowledge enabled by the missions, we are communicated a genuine participation in the personal properties of the Son and the Spirit: knowledge and love. Apart from such union with them, any knowledge is ignorance, and any love but melancholy. Only in the union with the two persons is our knowledge actualized (though not perfected) and our will moved (though not completed). What is now a tasting, however, is leading up to an actual banquet; this is the climax of the missions, and to this we can now turn.

---

46. A discussion of further interest is whether the Eucharist, as a participation in the humanity of Christ, could be further understood as a divine mission, or the prolongation of one. Reflection on the Eucharist from the perspective of the missions has been lacking, with some exceptions.

4

THE END OF THE MISSIONS

The Vision of God

THE CHRISTIAN TRADITION UNDERSTANDS THE CULMINAtion of the divine missions to be the return (*reditus*) of creatures to God. The end of our faith is not simply a human paradise, however grand, but perfect communion with God, where our proximity to him is described as seeing him face to face. The missions, however, already indicate the intimate presence of God in the indwelling of the Son and the Spirit. The life of grace is already a supernatural kind of life. But the whole creation anticipates a life of glory, whose signs we glimpse already, but which has not arrived yet. In the invisible missions, then, we have a foretaste of this life of glory. But, as a foretaste, this enjoyment of God will be dwarfed by our unencumbered vision in the afterlife.

A number of final questions present themselves at this point. Given the continuity between the life of grace and the life of glory provided by the supernatural presence of the Son and Spirit, how are we to understand the role of these missions in *disposing* us for glory? We have to probe here the precise continuity between the two lives, and whether the glory is something like an extrinsic reward or more like an intrinsic flowering of a supernatural principle already given to us. What is the nature of this vision of God, and how are the triune persons related to it? Does it consist in the contemplation of the divine essence, or of the divine persons, or both—how? Since God is spirit, what is the role of our bodies and of bodily sight in the beatific vision? Connected to the previous two questions is a final one: what is the role of the incarnate Son and his body in this vision?

It is fitting to discuss the beatific vision in this final chapter, since the character of the missions is illuminated by their end: the vision of God. We recognize that the topic of the vision of God is vast, and we commit only to highlighting those areas of convergence indicated by the questions above.

ON THE POSSIBILITY OF THE VISION

Scripture has much to say about the vision of God. In general, it affirms that no one can see God and live (Exod 33:20), despite episodes of proximity that are interpreted as seeing God (Gen 32:30; Judg 6:22; Isa 6:5). The rule of thumb has been to interpret these as theophanies whereby God presents himself in some created angelic form. Although in Exodus 33:11 we read that "the LORD used to speak to Moses face to face, as a man speaks to his friend," we must again interpret this theophanically, in light of Moses's request to see the glory of God (33:18) and God's refusal (33:20: "You cannot see my face, for man shall not see me and live").

The New Testament presents Christ, the incarnate Son, as the one who makes the invisible Father known: "No one has ever seen God; the only God, who is at the Father's side, he has made him known" (John 1:18; cf. John 6:46). Christ is "the image of the invisible God" (Col 1:15), the one in whom God may finally be seen, as he tells Philip: "Whoever has seen me has seen the Father" (John 14:9).

Yet, although Christ is the true image of God, as Philip's incomprehension demonstrates, the glory of God does not shine in the face of Christ with an immediacy that leaves no room for doubt—except perhaps in the case of the transfiguration. Without the illuminating light of faith, this glory may not be seen (Eph 1:17–19; Col 2:2; 2 Cor 4:4). It is by faith that we now see God in the face of Jesus Christ, as in a mirror, as Paul puts it (1 Cor 13:12), darkly or in obscurity, through an enigma (δι' ἐσόπτρου ἐν αἰνίγματι).

So even as Christ is the true image, we long for a seeing face to face. "For now we see in a mirror dimly, but then face to face. Now I know in part; then I shall know fully, even as I have been fully known" (1 Cor 13:12). Although a certain transformation, from glory to glory, is taking place even now, as we imperfectly behold the glory of the Lord (2 Cor 3:18), we anticipate a future and as yet unknown transformation when we shall see him in an unencumbered manner, as John puts it: "What we will be has not yet appeared; but we know that when he appears we shall be like him, because we shall see him as he is" (1 John 3:2).

The grand vision of the saints in glory presented by John in the Apocalypse repeats the same theme of seeing the face of Christ: "They will see his face, and His name will be on their foreheads" (Rev 22:4). The radiance of God's glory will shine on them and there will be no need for the sun, moon, or any other lamps (Rev 22:5; cf. Isa 60:20; Ps 36:9). The light is not simply the light of God, however, but also the light shining from the Lamb ("its lamp is the Lamb"—Rev 21:23).

To summarize, God's transcendence and holiness are indicated by the unapproachable light in which he dwells, which no man can see and live (1 Tim 6:16). But the saints, the pure in heart, are blessed, for they shall see God (Matt 5:8). A glimpse of God's glory is already seen in Christ, through faith alone, anticipating the full revelation, where God will be all in all and when we shall see everything in the light of God.

But what does it mean to see God? Two broad approaches to this question have emerged in the Christian tradition. We shall first examine an Eastern approach, which, taking its cues from the Greek fathers, will insist on the impossibility of seeing the divine essence, stressing instead the contemplation of the divine person in the uncreated energies of the Trinity. On the other hand, a Latin Thomistic tradition explains the beatific vision as a seeing of the divine essence itself, in the light of glory. Although the individual positions are much more nuanced than we can capture here, we shall paint with broad brush strokes in order to highlight the distinctness of the two approaches.

Orthodox Position

The Orthodox position on the vision of God has been shaped by its interaction with Platonism, Middle Platonism, and—very decisively—by the Trinitarian controversies with the Arians and with Eunomius. In general contours, it eschews an overly intellectualized approach, such as it thinks it finds in the Latin West; it stresses the trinitarian nature of the vision, and consequently it claims to be more christological and pneumatological.

Vladimir Lossky helpfully summarizes five distinctives of this approach as opposed to the scholastic tradition. First is the foundational nature of the conflict with Eunomius for the question of the knowledge of the divine nature; we will unpack this at more length in what follows. Secondly, by an appeal to the idea of "uncreated light," theologians such as Gregory Palamas sought to overcome the dualism between a purely intellectual light—such as the light of glory in the Catholic tradition—and a sensible light, a light that can be seen with bodily eyes. Eastern apophaticism is most clear at this point. The vision of God takes us beyond simple knowing, or simple seeing. When *hesychastic* monks[1] testify to seeing a divine light, such a light is not a mere "created effect," as the Western tradition prefers to understand any incursion of God in creation, but the very uncreated glory, *shekinah*, of God. Moreover, such a light is accessible even now. In distinction from the scholastic framework, where the beatific vision is reserved for the light of glory, since it entails an unmediated knowledge of the divine essence, Orthodoxy stresses the availability of such an experience for the wayfarers, but especially for the mystics, since it involves an arduous process of purification. The third characteristic assumption is the centrality of Christology. The image of the Father, even before the incarnation, is the Son. But this means that the Son himself is invisible in his own nature, just as the Father is invisible in his nature. Hence, the manifestation of the Son in the incarnation is not according to his being but in a mirror, through an enigma. The Orthodox expectation, then, focuses on the vision of Christ in the fullness of his divine glory: "Since God manifested himself by becoming man, we will see God in the humanity of Christ."[2] We will return to the centrality of the Christ for the beatific vision in the last section of this chapter. Fourthly, for the Eastern tradition, it is the reality of deification that frames the ultimate seeing face to face. The christological moment indicates the vision of God as the ascent made possible by the incarnation, yet through the Holy Spirit, which ultimately leads to seeing the glory of Christ, not as in a mirror but face to face. This is also the pneumatological moment. Finally, the transfiguration of Christ occupies an important role as a foretaste of our "Christoformic fate."[3] The exalted and deified humanity of Christ demonstrates that "not only the human *nous* of Christ, but also his soul and his body are transfigured by their participation in his Divinity."[4]

1. Hesychasm is a type of the monastic life in which practitioners engage in the practice of total prayer. The Hesychastic controversy of the fourteenth century concerned, more broadly, the relation between the body and the spirituality of God and, more specifically, the nature of the light seen by many such monks in the fulcrum of prayer.
2. Lossky, "Problème," 529.
3. Pseudo-Dionysius, *Divine Names*.
4. Lossky, "Problème," 534.

Lossky has called this a "perichoresis" or "energetic penetration of the created by the uncreated,"[5] and this is analogous to the persons that become "gods according to grace."[6]

We mention these things only in passing, but we will return to most of them at more length below. The first distinctive characteristic, however, bears most directly on our question, of the possibility of seeing God. How should one interpret the scriptural hope that one day we shall see God face to face? That we shall, as John puts it, see him as he is? It is axiomatic for the Orthodox that God's essence is unknowable—and that it remains unknowable even in the life of glory. This position was forged in the fires of the controversy with Eunomius—and like any position forged in the fire of controversy, it bears something of the contingency of the controversy itself. Like much trinitarian theology, many of its central concepts bear connotations by association.

Eunomius was a theologian in the lineage of Arius, who insisted on both the transcendence of God and—ironically—on the knowability of the divine essence. His philosophy of language distinguished between conventional names and essential names. Conventional names tell us nothing about the essence of the object, and they have no lasting value. Essential names, on the other hand, give us the very essence of the object itself. One of the essential names for God was *agennetos*, unbegotten. If this is so, and furthermore, if the Son is begotten, then the Son and the Father do not share the same essence. The Son is thus on the created side of the Father, being a production of the Father, the first and only unmediated creation of the Father.

In response, the Cappadocians, especially Basil and Gregory of Nyssa, supply their own understanding of the function of language. We know things through their operations, or energies, and not in their essence as such. This does not apply to God alone but to things in general, whose natures always transcend their manifestation. So we know God also in his works, or energies, and not in his being. Nevertheless, we can and should speak not only about the energies of God but about his *ousia*. Why? Because if we were to speak only of the energies of God, we would not be able to indicate the Trinity, since the energies of the Trinity are common to all the persons. Nevertheless, from the common energies of the persons we must ascend towards a contemplation of their personal identity.

---

5. Lossky, "Problème," 534.
6. Lossky, "Problème," 534.

The terms that we use to indicate their personal identity are themselves drawn from their energies, however. They do not grasp, as it were, the essence of God, which remains unknowable. Nevertheless, we move from *oikonomia* to *theologia* as two inseparable moments, just as God's essence and his energies are inseparable. In the economic energies of God we see a kind of flickering, so to speak, which leads us to wonder, to explore, to probe more deeply into the mystery of God's essence. It is precisely this probing that reveals such an essence to be of a trinitarian kind. Yet, in knowing the trinitarian persons, we do not know their essence. Instead, we learn to appreciate their relations. What Eunomius had not grasped is the possibility of relational names as a third category, in addition to conventional and essential names. These are terms that indicate the distinctions between the persons within the unity of the same simple substance.

The Cappadocians sow the seeds of the distinction between the essence and the energies of God. Later consolidated in the theology of Gregory Palamas, in the fires of yet another controversy, this distinction would become standard for the whole Eastern tradition. At the moment of the controversies with Eunomius, however, what gets consolidated is the notion that the essence of God remains unknowable.

So then what may be seen in the eschatological vision? Whatever "seeing him as he is" means, it may not mean that we shall see the divine essence itself. This, for the Orthodox, remains the infinite surplus behind the energies of God, ensuring both divine freedom[7] as well as his transcendence over creation. Whereas Eunomius separates between God's essence and his energies, and the West identifies them (God is pure act), the Cappadocians unite them without confusion. The divine energies are, as Dumitru Stăniloae puts it, not identical with his essence but surround it like an aura, like the radiance of the sun. The triad Essence-Persons-Energies replaces the Western diad of Essence-Persons.

Thus, in the vision of God, we move from the energies to an ever deeper contemplation of the persons, while the divine essence remains forever hidden. The essence and the persons are not two different realities, however. The distinction between them, while real, is not a separation. Each of the persons has the fullness of the divine essence. This enables the Orthodox to claim that the vision of God does not reach all the way down to the divine essence, yet without making it seem as if the essence is a fourth reality, beyond the persons themselves.

---

7. For more on this, see Vidu, "Triune Agency, East and West."

The Thomistic Position

Aquinas's position on the possibility of seeing God is elaborated in several places in the *Summa Theologica*, the *Summa contra gentiles*, and *De Veritate*. He discusses the possibility of the vision specifically in the *ST*, first under auestion 12 of the *prima pars*, to which we now turn. He first argues that the created intellect should be able to see the essence of God, for otherwise "the natural desire would remain void." He accepts a natural desire to see God, which is related to man's ultimate blessedness. Hence, "if we suppose that the created intellect could never see God, it would either never attain to beatitude, or its beatitude would consist in something else beside God; which is opposed to faith."[8] He is quick to stress, however, that seeing God is not the same as comprehending him! Additionally, as we shall see, whilst all saints will see the essence of God, there will be degrees of vision and levels of understanding of this essence. So we have here a superficial similarity between the Orthodox emphasis on the unavailability of the divine essence and the Thomist acknowledgement of its incomprehensibility. God continues to exceed every kind of knowledge.[9] Aquinas returns to the question of the comprehensibility of God in article 7 of the same question, where he explains that "God is called incomprehensible not because anything of Him is not seen; but because He is not seen as perfectly as He is capable of being seen."[10]

Aquinas returns to the same issue in the supplement, question 92, where he argues, apparently against the distinction between nature and energies, that the glory of God, which the saints are promised, is not different from his nature, and thus it is the very essence of God that will be seen by the saints. Aquinas anticipates a battery of objections, which we do not have sufficient space to present, much less discuss at this point. We shall, however, return to some of them in the next section on the manner of the vision.

The fundamental difficulty of seeing the essence of God is epistemological. Without getting into a very technical discussion, Aquinas's basic epistemology assumes that when some object is known, that object comes to exist in the knower under a particular likeness. The essence of the thing is *abstracted* from the thing itself, and, in conjunction with the *phantasms*,

---

8. Aquinas, *ST* I, q. 12, art. 1, *responsio*.
9. Aquinas, *ST* I, q. 12, art. 1, ad. 3.
10. Aquinas, *ST* I, q. 12, art. 7, ad. 2.

it becomes present to the knower. This assumes that the essence of the object is distinct from the existence of the object, such that there is no need for the thing itself to exist inside the knower. For example, in order for me to *know* a tree, it is not the tree itself that must pass through my mind, but just its essence, or form. We are already familiar with this notion from our discussion of causality. A form is that which makes the particular matter the thing that it is. Knowledge, for Aquinas, implies the ability to distill this form from the particular and to entertain it in one's mind, in conjunction with the sensory experience of that particular thing.

This obviously creates a problem for the knowledge of God. Given divine simplicity, God's essence is identical to his existence, so it is not possible to abstract some likeness or similitude of God. Thus, the form by which we know God is not God himself but some other created form or image of God—in which case we would not see God face to face. Or, this form really is God himself, in which case we risk making ourselves God, or we risk making God the form of some matter. We shall return at more length to these discussions.

Aquinas insists that the ground of the possibility of the vision of God's essence is the divine essence itself: "The vision whereby we shall see God in His essence is the same whereby God sees Himself, as regards that whereby He is seen, because as He sees Himself in His essence, so shall we also see Him."[11] In other words, God's essence itself becomes *that whereby* he is seen. A difference still remains, however, given that the power of the knower is infinitely smaller than God's own power of knowledge.

In summary, it appears that the Eastern suspicion of the scholastic vision of the divine essence is haunted by the specter of Eunomius, whose exaggerated intellectualism set the terms of the Orthodox reaction. Lossky and company continue to suspect that the West has abandoned the incomprehensibility of the divine essence. The Western doctrine of divine simplicity, which identifies God with his operations, comes perilously close to Eunomius's intellectualism. By contrast, for the Cappadocians, "instead of contemplation of the *ousia* it is here knowledge of the Trinity which constitutes the object of theology. Simplicity is no longer the dominating characteristic, since by discerning the internal relationships of the divine being reflection directs contemplation toward something which surpasses the intelligible *ousia* or super-intelligible unity."[12]

11. Aquinas, *ST* Suppl., q. 92, art. 1, ad. 1.
12. Lossky, *Vision of God*, 67.

For the West, the contemplation of the divine essence, as the end of the natural desire for God, must be possible. Man's happiness resides in it. For the East, on the other hand, sheer knowledge cannot by itself lead to beatitude, as Gregory of Nyssa points out: happiness does not consist simply in knowing God but in being united to God. The "seeing" that leads to beatitude is not mere intellectual seeing but surpasses it, passing through light into the divine darkness, where *theoria* ceases. Nyssen identifies this with love.[13]

It remains to be seen whether these Eastern critiques of Latin views of the beatific vision are entirely justified. To this end we must probe more deeply into the nature of the beatific vision in the Western account. Does it sufficiently respond to the following critiques: that it is an overly intellectualized vision; that it overlooks the centrality of Christ in the vision; that it lacks a pneumatological explication of the vision.

THE VISION AS THE TERMINUS OF THE MISSIONS

In answering the question of how the missions terminate in the beatific vision, we are in fact probing into the convertibility of the two. Our blessedness cannot be something merely given to us extrinsically, but it must be understood as the ultimate fruition of the missions themselves. The reason for this is as follows. Should the vision be only extrinsically connected to the temporal missions of the persons, the present life of grace would appear somewhat meaningless. However, an attempt to secure its significance *via* a theology of extrinsic merits would be very problematic from a Protestant standpoint suspicious of anything smacking of works-righteousness. The possibility of the vision must be understood as something that is established in the very life of grace, specifically through the two missions of the Son and Spirit, and not simply in the sense that the mission of the Son obtains objective salvation (atonement) and serves as the efficient or instrumental cause of the beatific vision, while the mission of the Spirit is to unite us to Christ through baptism. Rather, the two missions must be understood as vectors of our return to God and *intrinsically* aimed at the vision of God. This is what we must then probe in this section: what are the respective natures of the beatific vision and of the divine missions, such that the former is the fruition of the latter?

---

13. See Lossky, *Vision of God*, 71, referencing the "Sixth Homily on Beatitudes" by Nyssen.

What Is the Beatific Vision?

First, what is the nature of the beatific vision? The possibility of the vision was already discussed in the previous section. The Western tradition stresses that the beatific vision consists in the vision, though not in the comprehension of the divine essence. The Eastern tradition, conversely, rejects the vision of the divine essence, insisting instead on a continual deification by participation in the uncreated energies of God, a participation that is available already in the life of grace. Given such an account, for the East the current question does not even arise. There is no qualitative difference, so to speak, between the life of grace and the life of glory. The saints can already enjoy the divine uncreated light in moments of mystical ecstasy, and we already have a share in the divine energies. For Aquinas, on the other hand, the dichotomy between seeing darkly, as through a looking glass, and seeing face to face is at the forefront. Eastern theology imagines a constant and never-ending ascent towards ever greater deification, already commencing in this life. Catholic theology in particular emphasizes the radical novelty of a vision of the divine essence that is going to take place in an instant. However, it is the very novelty of the vision that requires the clarification of the role of the present missions. Let us turn to that.

Our Natural Epistemic Limitations

As we have seen, when Aquinas studies the possibility of the beatific vision, he encounters an epistemological difficulty. Knowledge presupposes a convertibility of the knower and the known, more specifically, between the capacity of the intellect and the nature of the known object. But given the infinite qualitative difference between God and the human intellect, the intellect cannot naturally know God. In the Angelic Doctor's framework, when an object is known, there isn't so much an intentional stretching out of the intellect towards the object, as much as a coming to be of the object in the intellect. In knowledge, specifically, the object is assimilated into the intellect through a form, a similitude, which is the intelligible species of the thing. When something is known, the intellect, which is up to that point in potency, comes to be in act with respect to that thing. To put it differently, the mind receives the thing itself according to its (the mind's) own powers.[14] The mind is informed by the similitude of the thing.

---

14. Aquinas, *ST* I, q. 12, art. 4.

In the vision of God, however, the intellect cannot be informed by a similitude, since it would necessarily be a similitude of an inferior order of things. Moreover, as we saw, given simplicity, one cannot abstract an essence of God from his existence—unlike created things, which are compounds of essence and existence. There is no "created similitude representing the divine essence as it really is."[15] Thus, God is not seen through some intermediary likenesses, as in this life, when we perceive God and understand God through analogical concepts, which bear some resemblance to God, since, as perfections, they ultimately derive from him. In this life, these perfections are faintly and imprecisely represented in our knowledge. In the life of glory, we shall glimpse them directly.

There is a natural affinity of the human mind for the kinds of substances that exist only in individual matter. We naturally know trees and stars, because these substances are like our souls, which are the form of a certain matter. This is the convertibility between our intellect and the "middle sized dry goods," as J. L. Austin calls them. This also means that the knowledge of our intellect is mediated through our senses, or our corporeal cognitive powers, which know only singular things, from which we ascend to the universal essence of the things. The two cognitive powers, sense and intellect, work together to produce our natural knowledge.

The Light of Glory

The knowledge of the divine essence, however, is not naturally accessible to us, for all the reasons detailed above, and therefore the intellect, Aquinas argues, must be raised above its natural powers; it must be prepared by a new disposition above its nature.[16] The *light of glory* is precisely this increase of the intellectual powers of the intellect, by which we are enabled to see God. This light is not a similitude in which we see God, not another image or even concept, but a perfection of the intellect, a strengthening of the intellect to make it capable of the vision. To put it differently, it is not a medium in which God is seen but one by which he is seen.[17]

We may thus think of the light of glory as a *created* enhancement of the intellect, but we must steer clear of the idea that it is something *in which* we see God. The light of glory is a created supernatural reality, and thus

---

15. Aquinas, *ST* I, q. 12, art. 2, resp.
16. Aquinas, *ST* I, q. 12, art. 5.
17. Aquinas, *ST* I, q. 12, art. 5, ad. 2.

something that is bestowed extrinsically upon the blessed. Without this light, the saints cannot see the divine essence. Its presence is what accounts for the radical disparity between the life of grace, where we see in the light of faith, and the life of glory, where we see in the light of glory. Let's test an analogy: the light of glory is like a microscope through which we can see a reality otherwise inaccessible to our senses, or like a telescope through which we may perceive faraway worlds. We do not see these new worlds *in* these instruments, only *through* them.

While this position gives a better account of the novelty of the eschatological seeing than the Eastern doctrine, it does introduce an extrinsic element (a created supernatural supplementing of the visual powers), which threatens the continuity between the divine missions and the beatific vision. It now appears that it is the light of glory, and not the visible and particularly the invisible missions, that leads to the vision of God. The question is now before us about the relation between the missions and the light of glory itself, since both entail created realities. We return to this question shortly, but we must touch now upon another aspect of this position.

Understanding God through His Own Essence

Aquinas adamantly affirms that the beatific vision consists in seeing the very essence of God. This is a position of momentous import. Such a vision of God is no longer mediated through created images, or even analogical images taken from creation. Whereas, as we have seen in relation to the Cappadocians, who hold that created knowledge of God takes place by a contemplation of God informed by an experience of his works in creation, the final vision sees God directly and without mediation. Now we have our backs turned towards God, and we know him through his works all around us. Then we shall see him face to face.

So what Aquinas is telling us is that we will see God as he sees himself! The audacity of this claim is staggering. We have here nothing less than the overcoming of the dualism between subject and object, between the knower and the known. Our knowledge of God will no longer employ human concepts, even concepts such as *trinity*, or *goodness*, or any other concepts, since these are harvested from the works of God in creation. Rather, we will find ourselves within God himself, as it were, knowing him through himself.

Aquinas explains this in the following way. Whereas in natural human knowledge the intelligible species of the thing known becomes the form of our intellect, making our intellect to be in act (or making actual a particular knowledge), in the vision of God, it is the very essence of God that takes the place of any similitude or intelligible species and forms our intellect. What Aquinas is doing here is pretty significant, and we must wrestle with these difficult concepts.

Recall for a moment our discussion of formal causality. In this type of causality, a thing is made to be what it is by the essence (or form) which is united to the matter and forms it. This particular dog, Bucky, is made to be the thing that he is by the form "canine," "dog," "dogness," which is made particular in this matter. Matter individualizes a particular form (which is universal). Just like Bucky is a real compound of form and matter, in knowledge we have a mental compound of form and matter. The matter is the passive intellect, which is made to be in act by the form it receives, which is the intelligible species.

Now, in natural knowledge, we do not receive the actual thing inside our minds (thankfully), but only an abstracted likeness. This is one symptom of the dualism of subject and object, generating all kinds of skepticisms: are we ever in touch with the real world? Do we ever know the things in themselves?—and a battery of other such questions. But in the beatific vision, if Aquinas is right, it is the very thing itself that makes our intellect to be in act. That is, our intellect is moved from potency to act by God. Our intellect is truly perfected in the sense that there is no more intellectual gap between the two. Understanding this with respect to Aquinas is crucial. It puts into perspective all claims about the intellectualism of the Doctor. The knowledge of God possessed by the blessed is not merely intellectual, because it presupposes an ontological union (without confusion, to be sure) between the knower and the known. It would not be too much of a stretch to claim that it is precisely the mystical union beyond knowledge to which the Eastern fathers allude.

The divine essence, writes Aquinas, is "the form whereby the intellect understands: and this will be the beatific vision. Hence the Master [Peter Lombard] says[18] that the union of the body with the soul is an illustration of the blissful union of the spirit with God."[19] What a beautiful analogy. Just as the soul forms a particular lump of flesh to be the body of a person,

18. Lombard, *Sentences: Book 2*, dist. 1, ch. 6.2.
19. Aquinas, *ST* Suppl., q. 92, art. 1, *responsio*.

standing in a most intimate relation to it, God is most intimately present to our intellect. One might say that the intellect has been brought to participate in the very self-knowledge of God. Not that God will know himself through our intellects, which gets things backwards ontologically, but that our intellects know through God's intellect. God's intellect is not perfected by ours; ours are perfected by God's.

Is Rahner Right after All?

The perceptive reader might have realized that we are now apparently affirming precisely what we decisively rejected earlier: that God may not become the formal cause of anything. So why should it be acceptable to say this in the case of the beatific vision? The problem with the notion of formal cause is that God enters into composition with matter, resulting in a new unity, whereby God himself ends up being dependent on matter. However, the actualization of the passive intellect that takes place in knowledge is not a real composition but rather a mixed relation: the intelligible species that becomes the form of the knowledge is not constituted, but it constitutes the knowledge. Unlike in hylomorphic compounds, where the matter becomes constitutive of the very nature of the form, in mixed relations this does not happen. The human intellect is made to be in act by the very essence of God. The divine essence becomes the form by which the intellect understands, yet without becoming one in being with the intellect; the two become one only in the act of understanding.[20]

As we have seen, we shall see him as he sees himself. Aquinas further explains that we shall not only see him but also see and understand the things that God sees.[21] All things will have a clarity and a transparency to God's final purpose for them. Creation will be translucent to God; things will wear their divine purposes on their sleeves. At this point another worry

---

20. Aquinas, *ST*, Suppl, q. 92, art. 1, ad. 8.

21. First Cor 13:12 says, "Then I shall know fully, even as I have been fully known." I shall know fully precisely through God's own knowledge of myself. Although Aquinas denies (*ST* I, q. 12, art. 8) that the saints will know everything that God knows, and that the expanse of this knowledge depends on the sharpness of their comprehension of God (which will vary), he does accept that everyone who will see the divine essence will see in God and know "everything that belongs to the perfection of the intellect, namely the species and the genera of things and their types" (*ST* I, q. 12, art. 8, ad. 4). Aquinas denies that all saints will know particulars in the way that God does, since the knowledge of particulars does not belong to the natural desire of the intellect.

arises: however grand this picture may seem, where in all this is the Trinity? If the center of the beatific vision is the contemplation of the divine essence, have we reverted back to the neo-Platonic henad, beyond all differentiation and beyond Trinity? In this magnificent cathedral one can definitely hear the echo of the Eastern critique to the effect that the most important thing has been lost from sight, namely the relations between the Father, Son, and the Holy Spirit. This adds to the first critique, namely that there is a dichotomy between the life of grace and the life of glory, where in fact there should be more continuity. Why does the Trinity all of a sudden quiesce in Aquinas's beatific vision? Why, after the whole life of grace has been described in terms of the missions of the Son and the Spirit, visible and invisible, is the life of glory described in almost exclusively essentialist terms? Shouldn't heaven be primarily about the enjoyment of the personal fellowship with the Father, the Son, and the Spirit? We note here the convergence of the two critiques: (a) that there should be more continuity between the beatific vision and the divine missions in the life of grace; and (b) that there should be more attention to the Trinity, Christology, and even pneumatology in the life of glory. We will begin to tackle these issues together, first by engaging with Rahner's stimulating proposals.

We have already peeked into Rahner's theological project and his notion of quasi-formal causality. It is no accident that he works towards that idea of a quasi-formal self-communication precisely from the direction of the beatific vision. In this vision, he suggests, we already glimpse the possibility of a new relationship to God, which is not simply an accidental modification of our current relation. Rahner critiques the priority of created grace in our understanding of the divine missions. As we have seen, the notion of created grace pivots as an inseparable operation of the whole Trinity and does not reveal a distinct relation to just one of the trinitarian persons. In grace, then, the Christian is related to God along the same lines of efficient causality.

But, as we have just seen in Aquinas, in the beatific vision, we appear to have a relationship to God such that God is no longer extrinsic to us, and thus not simply in terms of efficient causality. True, the light of glory remains a created disposition, and thus it is an aspect of inseparable operations. But this light of glory disposes us for such a union with God, such that God's essence becomes *the form of our intellect*. This takes us beyond sheer efficient causality (whereby the cause remains extrinsic to the effect) to formal causality (where the cause is internal and intrinsic to the effect—just as "dogness" is intrinsic to Bucky). Rahner then argues that this possibility in fact demonstrates that all the strictly supernatural realities that we know are expressing a formal relationship to God, what he calls "a taking up into the ground (*forma*)."[22] What are these supernatural relations? The incarnation is one of them: here the Son becomes the ontological principle of the subsistence of a finite human nature. In the beatific vision, similarly, we have in the divine essence the ontological principle of a finite knowledge of God.

Thus, Rahner wants to stress the continuity that exists between the life of grace and glory. In the life of grace, too, we have in fact a relationship of quasi-formal causality whereby certain created realities (the human nature of Christ, charity, knowledge) are formed by the divine persons (in the divine missions), thus anticipating the final union with God in the beatific vision. Thus, "the possession of the Pneuma (and thus primarily uncreated grace) is conceived in Scripture as the homogenous germ and commencement of the beatific vision."[23] Note the language of *homogenous commencement*. In other words, the beatific vision is not qualitatively different from the possession of the Spirit, although the former remains "still concealed and still to unfold."[24]

The difficulties associated with Rahner's account of quasi-formality have been already enunciated. One must only note at this point the difference between the divine essence becoming the form of the intellect, on the one hand, and the divine persons becoming the form of either knowledge (mission of the Son) or charity (mission of the Holy Spirit). Rahner is arguing for what is the case now in the life of grace from what will be the case in the life of glory. As in the case of Orthodoxy, it is incumbent upon him to show of what consists the qualitative difference between "as in a mirror" and "face to face." Rahner minimizes the difference and downplays it as just progress, or a kind of quantitative difference.

Surely, however, it is not the same thing to say, with Aquinas, that the divine *essence* becomes the form of our intellect and, with Rahner, that a divine *person* becomes the quasi-form of some created reality. A person is already an incommunicable mode of the divine essence; it is, so to speak, already a particular. So there is at the very least an equivocation here. But it would go beyond the aims of this little book to enter too deeply into such

---

22. Rahner, "Some Implications of the Scholastic Concept," 334.
23. Rahner, "Some Implications of the Scholastic Concept," 334.
24. Rahner, "Some Implications of the Scholastic Concept," 335.

a technical conversation. We have noted the desire of Rahner to find more continuity between the two lives: of glory and grace; of faith and vision.

Life of Grace and Life of Glory

But the two lives are in fact very different from one another. Aquinas addresses the possibility of seeing God in this life in *ST*.[25] He stresses that in this life we can see God only by images. Because the mode of knowledge follows the mode of the knower, and because in this life our soul has its being in corporeal matter, we are naturally capable of knowing what has a form in matter. While it is possible that our souls are supernaturally raptured and given the light of glory to behold the essence of God even in this life, this does not belong to the normality of the life of grace. And it is precisely because we see God only in created images that we relate to him through his inseparable operations in creation, that our relation to God in this life is through created grace. The formality of the divine missions, as we have seen, are certain created means, or simply created grace.

Thus Aquinas would indeed stress some continuity between this life and the next: in faith we are disposed to enjoy the divine persons through the created gifts of knowledge and love, which are products of the essential (and inseparable) activity of God. In glory, our intellect shall be elevated through the created means of the light of glory, which, however, will dispose us to behold the divine essence.

Doesn't Aquinas, however, fail to deliver on his promise? If created grace disposes us to experience the persons distinctly, why is it that in the beatific vision we contemplate the essence? Why is Aquinas mum on the much-expected experience of the persons? The key to this puzzle is to remember that persons, for Aquinas, are subsisting relations within the divine essence. To be distinctly related to a divine person is not to be related to a distinct essence but rather to experience (as we have seen in the previous chapter) the personal property of that person. The persons are present in a mission as distinct terms in virtue of their exemplar causality. I am distinctly related to the person of the Son, because I begin to exemplify his personal property as Word. Similarly, when I begin to exhibit the personal property of the Spirit, Love, he comes to dwell inwardly in me. This is precisely the theology of the invisible missions, which Aquinas helpfully spells out in terms of exemplar causality.

25. Aquinas, *ST* I, q. 12, art. 11.

To rehearse it, by the gifts of created grace, the believer is disposed to know and to love God. He is disposed to experience the persons not as a future reality but as a present event. The believer is truly related to the Son distinctly in the sense that knowledge of God takes root within her. She is also personally related to the Spirit in that she now loves God habitually. Thus, the missions of the divine persons take place by way of a modification of the operations of the believer, by an infusion of knowledge and love, which, in fact, are the formalities of the two indwellings.

This is not mere head knowledge, but it is truly experiential. The believer relates to the persons not from a distance, as it were, but by being imprinted with their personal property. Now, in the life of grace, this personal property of the Son is imprinted through faith, and through created similitudes (e.g., the human nature of Christ), through human concepts that make the Son present only dimly and imperfectly. That is, even if it is truly the Son who is present through the form of knowledge, this knowledge is imperfect but proportionate to the powers of the intellect that haven't been enhanced by the light of glory.

Aquinas specifically connects the idea of being formed into the image of the Trinity with vision and thus knowledge, echoing the correlation made by John: "When he appears we shall be like him, because we shall see him as he is" (1 John 3:2). In question 93 or the *prima pars*, he distinguishes between the image of God as natural aptitude, as habit, and as actuality and perfection (art. 4). He argues that when we know God and love him the image of God is formed in us: "It is at the level of action that the image of God in the soul is grasped first and in its principal way, inasmuch as starting from the knowledge we possess, we form, by thinking, a word, and, springing from that, our love."[26]

The Angelic Doctor explains that human beings do not simply possess the image as a thing, but rather they enact and perfect this image as they turn to God in knowledge and love. Such an image is not simply reflected in any activity of the mind, as Augustine also argues, but specifically when the mind is turned to God in love. In this way, God is the end of creatures. As D. J. Merriell puts it, "Man reflects the divine Trinity not merely as a mirror reflects a thing set to some distance from it, but as an actor who imitates the character he plays by entering into his character's life."[27]

---

26. Aquinas, *ST* I, q. 12, art. 11.

27. Donald J. Merriell, *To the Image of the Trinity*, as cited in Torrell, *Spiritual Master*, 89.

The indwelling Trinity restores the *imago Dei*.[28] Thus, in the life of grace, we are being remade into the image of the Trinity. This takes place precisely through our operations of knowledge and love. H. F. Dondaine puts it remarkably well:

> The return of the rational creature is achieved in the union of knowledge and love with God, our Object. Thus the whole cycle of temporal processions is completed; it is the goal of the whole history of the world: to show to rational creatures the intimate glory of the divine Persons. This union of the soul to the Triune God is begun, at least, on the level of habitus, at the very first infusion of grace, with the dowry of virtues and gifts that equip the soul for acts proportionate to the divine object. This union is realized gradually in imperfect acts of grasping God in the life of the Christian here below. It expands finally into the fulfilled vision in the beatific vision, which is a perfect and unchangeable act. All during this process, God gives himself in his three Persons, makes himself present to the soul, in a real and substantial presence, which bears the name Indwelling; presence of an Object to be grasped by experience ... of whom the definitive possession and enjoyment are fully operative only in the blessed vision, but of whom the progressive appropriations roughly attempted here below respond fully to the invisible missions of the Son and the Holy Spirit.[29]

The continuity is real and significant. Even in this life, through the indwelling persons, we are made to know and to love God habitually. In the life to come, we shall know and love God actually and perfectly. In this life, our knowledge is through similitudes and enigmas, as through a glass, darkly. In the life to come, we shall see him face to face, without mediation—through himself. In both lives, we enjoy the divine persons through their created gifts of knowledge and love. In this life, however, this knowledge is mediated by faith; and our love is made imperfect by our imperfect knowledge.

Aquinas rightly concludes that there is a direct implication between seeing the divine essence and becoming like him! "For God Himself understands his own substance through His own essence; and this is his felicity."[30]

---

28. Torrell states that Aquinas's "teaching about the indwelling Trinity is the crowning achievement of the teaching about the image of God" (Torrell, *Spiritual Master*, 92).

29. Dondaine, "Bulletin de Théologie," 437–38, as cited in Torrell, *Spiritual Master*, 100.

30. Aquinas, *Summa contra gentiles*, 51.6.

The process of regaining the likeness of God that commences in the divine missions is thus fulfilled at the eschatological banquet, when we shall enjoy God and share in his happiness.

Contemplating the Essence or the Persons?

But what about the beatific experience of the Trinity? We have noted Aquinas's silence on this topic and the Eastern critique of this position. However, on the basis of what has been thus far said, the solution is relatively straightforward. As subsistent relations within the divine essence, the divine persons are not separate substances that can be contemplated diversely. The Son is the Image that proceeds in God's essential activity of knowing himself and everything else. The Spirit is love proceeding, which emerges out of the essential activity of self-love, ordered to self-knowledge. Therefore, to behold God as he beholds himself is essentially to glimpse precisely the essential activities in conjunction with which the persons proceed from one another! Far from being an unfulfilled promise, the experience of the Trinity is now perfected, absent the encumberment of created concepts and images.

It may be said that the missions provide us with a foretaste of the eschatological banquet. Our happiness is not complete, because our knowledge (and thus our love) is not complete. To this we should add a point that contributes to our understanding of the continuity between grace and glory. According to Aquinas, although all the blessed shall see the divine essence, no one will fully comprehend it, but there will be degrees of comprehension as well. The difference in the extent of the vision of God will be determined by the degree of virtue a soul has acquired. Aquinas appeals to John 14:2, "In my Father's house are many rooms." What determines the different "degrees of glory" is the different power of vision that the blessed will have—even though they shall all contemplate the same object, God. "And so, of those who see Him, one may see His substance more or less than another, depending on whether one is more or less near to Him."[31] Aquinas appeals to the intrinsic correlation of virtue and happiness to demonstrate that the manner in which a person has been disposed for the vision of God in this life determines the *depth*, so to speak, of his beatific vision. He argues that "not all intellectual substances are disposed with equal perfection to the end; some, in fact, are more virtuous than others, and others less, and virtue

---

31. Aquinas, *Summa contra gentiles*, 58.2.

is the road to felicity. So, there must be diversity within the divine vision: some seeing the substance more perfectly; others, less perfectly."[32]

If this is true, then what accounts for the beatific vision is not simply the light of glory, extrinsically bestowed, and a matter of efficient causality. In addition to the light of glory, the disposition achieved by the creature through grace determines the extent of her reward in the beatific vision.

We have argued that there is a clear continuity between the life of grace and the life of glory, or between the divine missions and the beatific vision. Although the beatific vision requires the efficient elevation of our intellect through the light of glory, the divine missions prepare us and dispose us for the vision of the divine essence. Additionally, in response to the important worry of Eastern theologians that the vision of the divine essence places the Trinity itself in the latter's shadow cone, the vision of the divine essence necessarily entails a vision of the divine persons. In this consists our happiness, something which we now can taste only in faith.

THE PLACE OF CHRIST IN THE BEATIFIC VISION

It must not be supposed that, since the beatific vision consists in the beholding of the divine essence, the incarnate Son plays no part in it. In a greater or lesser detail, the major Christian traditions ascribe to Christ an ongoing role in the eschatological vision. This final section summarizes various explanations of his place in relation to the blessedness of the saints. This will form a fitting conclusion to our discussion of the conductivity of the divine missions to the beatific vision. It will be seen that such a seeing is not only *instrumentally* enabled by Christ, in the sense of his redemptive work, but that Christ continues to be *materially* part of the very content of that vision.

One of the ways in which the missions are related to the vision is that they dispose us, they prepare us for it. Since the vision of God takes place by way of an elevation of our intellect, even in this life, through the Son and the Spirit, there takes place a lightening of our intellect, where it gradually sheds all unnecessary ballast and becomes accustomed to rise to spiritual realities. In a certain sense, in this life we reacquire a lost taste for heavenly realities. Although we naturally desire God, by sin our taste has been corrupted, so that we no longer naturally appreciate spiritual realities.

---

32. Aquinas, *Summa contra gentiles*, 58.4.

THE END OF THE MISSIONS

Cabasilas on Developing a Taste for Eternity

Nicolaus Cabasilas's *Life in Christ* beautifully explains that in this life we develop the spiritual senses with which we shall experience Christ in the next. Stressing the centrality of Christ in the heavenly consummation, he explains that in order to enjoy that life, one must have developed a sense for it. "If the life to come were to admit those who lack the faculties and senses necessary for it, it would avail to nothing for their happiness, but they would be dead and miserable living in that blessed and immortal world."[33] The present and the yet-to-come are not simply linearly related, but they mix. There are signs and incursions of the life to come here and now. The eschatological reality of our new beings is created in this life and perfected in the next: "It is this world which is in travail with that new inner man which is 'created after the likeness of God' (Eph. 4:24). When he has been shaped and formed here he is thus born perfect into that perfect world which grows not old."[34]

According to Cabasilas, the sacraments in particular are the portals that usher the future into the present. Through baptism, we are engrafted into the body of Christ, and he appropriates our functions, transforming them, renewing them, and making them functions of his own body. We thus learn to see through Christ's eyes, to have the mind of Christ (Phil 2:5; 1 Cor 2:16), to act in the power of Christ (John 14:12), to speak as Christ (2 Cor 13:3)—in sum, we learn to act as the body of Christ (1 Cor 12:27).

The Eucharist sustains our life as members of this body, since from the head the rest of the body draws life (Col 1:18). Cabasilas notes a connection between the Eucharist and the heavenly banquet: "One body is the power of the table, one the Host in both worlds. The one world is the wedding feast with the Bridegroom Himself, the other the preparation for that wedding feast. Accordingly, those who depart this life without the Eucharistic gifts will have nothing for that life. But those who have been able to receive the grace and preserve it have entered into the joy of their Lord."[35] One might say that in the Eucharist, our taste for the heavenly Christ is developed. The sacramental elements not only sustain us in this life, being like Frodo's *lembas* in Tolkien's *The Lord of the Rings*, the *panis viatorum*, the food of pilgrims that sustains them on their journey. We misunderstand the Eucharist

---

33. Cabasilas, *Life in Christ*, 43.
34. Cabasilas, *Life in Christ*, 44.
35. Cabasilas, *Life in Christ*, 148.

if we think of it in terms of survival. Theologically speaking, it is not instrumental in justification. More appropriately, it must be understood as diet, as the kind of food that prepares our bodies for something other than mere survival. In the Eucharist, we are prepared to regard all nourishment from the perspective of the eschatological banquet and thus prepare ourselves for it, anticipating it, learning to long for it. In it, our natural desire for food is subordinated and transfigured into a desire for the supernatural food of Christ's body.

Aquinas on the Vision of Christ

The vision of Christ also has pride of place in Aquinas's understanding of the beatific vision. Despite his stress on the spiritual contemplation of the divine essence, which does not take place by bodily vision, there does remain a role for the latter. He explains[36] that, although "it will be impossible for [the intellect] to see the Divine essence as an object of direct vision; yet it will see it as an object of indirect vision, because on the one hand the bodily sight will see so great a glory of God in bodies, especially in the glorified bodies and most of all in the body of Christ." He then explains that "our body will have a certain beatitude from seeing God in sensible creatures; and especially in Christ's body."[37]

As resurrected bodies, our intellectual vision is accompanied by a bodily vision, which, however, does not access the divine essence directly, while it will see its glory reflected in everything else. These must not be imagined as two separate sightings, since the saints will have the divine essence constantly as their direct object of vision. In the same vision, the saints in heaven will see the divine essence and everything else through that essence.[38] The two will be inseparable, though distinct, from one another.

It is notable that Aquinas ties our beatitude to seeing God in Christ's body. Earlier he made the same connection: "Human beings are led to beatitude through the humanity of Christ . . . and so it was necessary that that knowledge which consists in the vision of God be most found most excellently in Christ, because a cause must always be more potent than

---

36. Aquinas, *ST* Suppl., q. 92, art. 2, *responsio*.
37. Aquinas, *ST* Suppl., q. 92, art. 2, ad. 6.
38. As we have seen, Aquinas allows at a minimum that all the blessed will have this knowledge of the species and genera of God's creation.

what is caused."[39] In this context Aquinas is concerned to argue that Christ possesses the beatific vision as man, and not simply in his divine nature. We have already seen that Aquinas ascribes to the humanity of Christ an instrumental role in our reception of all divine graces. In this case, too, if the beatific vision is essential to our blessedness, it must come to us through Christ's humanity as well. Now, this may only be taken to demonstrate that Christ's humanity is instrumental in getting us to that beatific vision, but it does not mediate the very content of that vision.

This impression is mistaken, as can be seen from Aquinas's discussion of the heavenly priesthood of Christ. In *ST* III, question 22, article 5, in response to the first objection, he states that "the saints who will be in heaven will have no further need to receive expiation through Christ's priesthood; but now, having been expiated, they will need to be consummated through Christ himself, on whom their glory depends." Gaine interprets "glory" as seeing God: "It seems to me that Aquinas may be saying that this act itself in heaven 'depends' causally on Christ's humanity."[40] He points out that Aquinas immediately refers to Rev 21:23 about the Lamb being the lamp, which he had already interpreted as the light of glory in the *prima pars*. Gaine explains that this is consistent with the role of Christ's humanity in relation to grace. Even our grace we receive because Christ first received it, and it pours out from him to us. This applies, as we have seen, to the Holy Spirit as well, who comes to us precisely as the Spirit of Christ, upon his ascension.

Some commentators have suggested that Aquinas is not as explicit as he might have been about the mediation of the beatific vision itself through the humanity of Christ. This is certainly true. But such a view is at least consonant with Aquinas's overall thought.[41] The fact that the humanity of Christ continues to play a central role in our beatific vision is asserted with particular force by John Owen and Jonathan Edwards.

John Owen on the Vision of Christ

In *Christologia*,[42] Owen considers the present state of Christ under three heads: the glorification of his human nature, his mediatory exaltation, and

39. Aquinas, *ST* III, q. 9, art. 2.
40. Gaine, "Beatific Vision," 123–24.
41. Gaine, "Beatific Vision," 119.
42. Owen, *Glory of Christ*.

the exercise and discharge of his office in the state of things. Here Owen is concerned to contrast Christ's glorified humanity and ours. One contrast is between the *immediate* communication of all divine benefits from his divine nature to his human nature, on the one hand, and, on the other, a communication to us "by an external efficiency of power."[43] This is true not only in this life, but "unto all eternity. It will be by what he *worketh in us* by his Spirit and power. There is no other way of the emanation of virtue from God unto any creature."[44] This is quite significant, in that Owen continues to insist that the Son's benefits flow to the believer—even in heaven—through the mediation of Spirit and power! Owen seems to be anticipating Rahner's attempt to eschew efficient causality and undercuts that move by insisting that even in heaven, we will receive everything from God through his Spirit and by his *work* in us.

But what about the direct vision of the divine essence? It is not that Owen denies it, as we shall see, but he stresses the centrality of Christ in that vision itself. The blessed "behold *openly* and *plainly* the whole glory of God, all the characters of it, illustriously manifesting themselves in him, in what he is, in what he hath done, in what he doth."[45] The beatific vision does not make the human Christ redundant: "The person of Christ, in and by his human nature, shall be forever the *immediate head of the whole glorified creation*. God having gathered all things unto a head in him, the knot or centre of that collection shall never be dissolved. We shall never lose our relation unto him, nor he his unto us."[46]

But the vision of Christ is not idle in the shadow of the beatific vision. It is not simply a kind of afterglow, or an effect of the vision itself. Owen seems to stress that the vision itself is mediated by Christ's humanity. He affirms that "he shall be *the means and way of communication* between God and his glorified saints for ever."[47] Whatever these communications, "they shall all be made in and through the person of the Son, and the human nature therein. That tabernacle shall never be folded up, never laid aside as useless."[48]

---

43. Owen, *Glory of Christ*, 240.
44. Owen, *Glory of Christ*, 240.
45. Owen, *Glory of Christ*, 242.
46. Owen, *Glory of Christ*, 271.
47. Owen, *Glory of Christ*, 271.
48. Owen, *Glory of Christ*, 271.

It is important to understand as carefully as possible the logical role of the vision of Christ's humanity. Owen appears to claim that God will be seen through the humanity of Christ. This appears to directly contradict Aquinas's position that the vision of God is not mediated through any created forms, whether intellectual or bodily. On the other hand, Owen clearly understands that the vision of God cannot take place by bodily organs. This dilemma appears to be clarified in his meditations on *The Glory of Christ*. In the final two chapters of that book, Owen contrasts the life of faith with the life of vision. He stresses that our vision of Christ in heaven is "immediate, direct, intuitive" and that "the *object* of it will be *real* and *substantial*. Christ himself, in his own person, with all his glory, shall be continually with us, before us, proposed unto us."[49]

But then Owen clearly shows that the priority does not belong to a visible contemplation of his humanity. Although we also see with our bodily eyes, "principally . . . this vision is intellectual. It is not, therefore, the mere human nature of Christ that is the object of it, but his divine person, as that nature subsisteth therein."[50] The following explanation cannot be clearer: "This beholding of the glory of Christ given him by his Father, is, indeed, subordinate unto the ultimate vision of the essence of God. What that is we cannot well conceive; only we know that the 'pure in heart shall see God.' But it has such an immediate connection with it, and subordination unto it, as that without it we can never behold the face of God as the objective blessedness of our souls. For he is, and shall be to eternity, the only means of communication between God and the church."[51]

Thus, for Owen, the vision of the humanity of Christ is necessarily presupposed by, yet subordinated to, the intellectual vision of the divine essence. It is not that the humanity of Christ *mediates* the divine vision (here Owen's language is misleading) as much as it is a *consequent condition* of the vision. That is, once you have the vision of the divine essence, you necessarily also see the humanity of Christ in all its glory. We may speculate whether this is what Owen had in mind when he wonders whether in the beatific vision we may understand the mystery of the incarnation.[52] But all this is consistent with a Chalcedonian understanding of Christology, such that the human nature subsists only in the Son. Thus, only by first

---

49. Owen, *Glory of Christ*, 378.
50. Owen, *Glory of Christ*, 379.
51. Owen, *Glory of Christ*, 385–86.
52. Owen, *Glory of Christ*, 239.

attending to the divine person of the Son may one truly understand the human nature itself. The same priority that we have observed in the case of the mission, where the created effect is subordinated to the procession, is applicable in heaven. Owen may be saying that in heaven the mission still continues. We are still brought into the love of the Father through the Son and in the Spirit. The Son continues to mediate our relationship to the Father. Only now, in heaven, that is, we no longer see darkly, as in a mirror. The union that the mission indicates has not dissolved. The Son still holds his human nature—and us in it. He is still coming forth from the Father. He is still on mission, as it were. The difference is that we now behold this mission from the opposite direction. By having a vision of the divine essence, we gaze on the mission downwards, as it were, rather than, dazed and blinded, upwards. We no longer gaze upon the sun, resulting in the blurring of our vision of everything else. Rather, we look down from the sun and see everything in its light. The missions of the Son and Spirit do not end upon the commencement of the beatific vision. The Son continues to come forth from the Father in a human nature. The Spirit continues to be poured into our hearts as the love of the Father and the Son. But then we shall see face to face, we shall see God as he is, and only then shall we truly know the missions.

Jonathan Edwards on the Physical Vision of Christ

Jonathan Edwards brings out the christological and pneumatological mediation of the beatific vision with particular force in *The Portion of the Righteous*. With Owen he, too, stresses the centrality of Christ in the beatific vision. Edwards writes that "the saints in heaven shall see God. [They shall] not only see that glorious city, and the saints there, and the glorified body of Christ; but they shall see God himself."[53] This includes the sight of Christ: "The sight of Christ [glorified], which has already been spoken of, is not here to be excluded because he is a divine person. The sight of him in his divine nature therefore belongs to the beatifical vision."[54] But Edwards seems to reject any sight of light. "We have no reason to think that there is any such thing as God's manifesting himself by any natural glorious appearance that is the symbol of his presence in heaven, any otherwise than

---

53. Edwards, "Excerpt," 118.
54. Edwards, "Excerpt," 118.

by the glorified body of Christ."[55] This seems to be more of a rejection of the uncreated light of the Hesychasts than the "light of glory" of the Western tradition, which is not a visible light, at any rate. But Edwards insists on (what appears to be) the sufficiency of beholding Christ with bodily eyes. Since Christ is a divine person, "the saints do actually see a divine person with bodily eyes, and in the same manner as we see one another." Moreover, "there is no need of God the Father's manifesting himself in a distinct glorious form, for he that sees the Son sees the Father, as Christ has said."[56]

Edwards sees little need for additional concepts, such as "light of glory," for example. The manner of seeing God is simply through communion with Christ:

> The manner in which they shall see and enjoy God: and that is as having communion with Christ therein. The saints shall enjoy God as partaking with Christ of his enjoyment of God: for they are united to him, and are glorified and made happy in the enjoyment of God as his members. As the members of the body do partake of the life and health of the head, so the saints in glory shall be happy as partaking of the blessedness of the Son of God. They, being in Christ, shall partake of the love of God the Father to Christ. And as the Son knows the Father, so they shall partake with him in his sight of God, as being as it were parts of him. As he is in the bosom of the Father, so are they in the bosom of the Father. As he has immense joy in the love of the Father, so have they, every one of them in their measure, the same joy in the love of the Father.[57]

Since we are already in Christ, Edwards seems to say, this will suffice for our contemplation of the Father. This includes a pneumatological mediation as well: "The means by which God shall grant this vision of himself . . . is the Holy Ghost. As 'tis by the Holy Ghost that a spiritual sight of God is given in this world, so 'tis the same Holy Spirit by which a beatifical vision is given of God in heaven. . . . They shall have this beatifical vision of God, because they will be full of God, filled with the Holy Spirit of God."[58]

Edwards's position need not be interpreted in antinomy with Aquinas's and Owen's. The former, especially, affirms—even if only tentatively—the instrumentality of Christ's own beatific vision in ours. Aquinas, too, would

---

55. Edwards, "Excerpt," 119.
56. Edwards, "Excerpt," 119.
57. Edwards, "Excerpt," 121.
58. Edwards, "Excerpt," 121.

stress that it is through partaking of Christ, because of our inclusion in him, that we share all his beatitude. And if it may be supposed that the beatitude of Christ entails the light of glory—if, that is, we are convinced by Aquinas's epistemological arguments about its necessity—then by implication our own beatific vision implies a light of glory, if indirectly, as Christ's own light of glory. On this reading, what Edwards is stressing is that all of these (perhaps necessary) elevations and formalities have already taken place in the deification and transfiguration of Christ's humanity. No additional preparation is needed of the human being than Christ's own preparation, no additional perfecting than Christ's own perfecting (Heb 2:10).

CONCLUSION

The beatific vision represents the glorious fulfilment of all human desire. The enjoyment of God for which we have been created consists in perfected knowledge and love, in union with the Father, Son, and Holy Spirit. We have shown how the life of glory stands in continuity with the life of grace. The missions of the Son and Spirit prepare us for our beatitude in that they develop in us the taste for God. Without this taste for God, the eschatological banquet would be spoiled, and the presence of God would become a torment.[59] Our beatitude, then, is an intrinsic consequence of this earthly preparation. Not only are the missions conduits to the vision, but the incarnate Christ will have pride of place in this vision. We have shown how this is not at odds with the spiritual nature of the vision or with the Western claim that we shall see (without fully comprehending) the divine essence. Neither is this focus on the seeing of the divine essence at odds with the three-personal fellowship. The vision of the essence does not obscure the persons, which are, in fact, just the essence regarded from a relational perspective. By seeing the essence, we not only see God as he sees himself, i.e., through his essence, but we also see everything else in that same act. Consequently, our vision of all created things, persons, nature, and, supremely, Christ himself is going to be from that lofty vantage point of the divine understanding.

---

59. It was noted that this was Cabasilas's position, and it leads to the intriguing possibility of construing hell as not itself lacking the presence of God—who is omnipresent, after all—but rather as a place for those irretrievably allergic to God. A similar position has been developed by Stump, "Dante's Hell."

CONCLUSION

LIKE ABBOTT'S *FLATLAND*, THE CONCEPTUALITY OF *MISSION* IS forcing us to think beyond the ordinary, often leading to a defamiliarization of our most habitual assumptions. While the category itself is not new, it has often lain dormant. Protestant theology (and Eastern Orthodoxy, though for different reasons) has not traditionally availed itself of this category in its trinitarian theology. By recovering and renewing a theology of the divine missions, we are suggesting a more *ontological* approach to the economy of salvation, one that strives to see both the immediate operations and created effects of God but also what is present behind them and within them: a new manner of divine presence. The forensic, judicial approach emphasized by the Reformers need not be threatened by the heavier ontological account. There is no need to pit this approach against a so-called *participationist* account. Nevertheless, inevitably an approach to theology that foregrounds the divine missions will situate the forensic on the background of the ontological, whether we call it participationist or not. Failure to be cognizant of the missions, however, is akin to the myopic fixation on what is right in front of us, but this results in a knowledge that lacks depth. Like Flatlanders puzzling about the misbehaving circle, we may fail to realize that is a manifestation of a transcendent reality.

Attentiveness to the category of mission lends theology a greater depth of field. Some may object that such a theology fails to attend to the real humanity of Christ, focusing instead on a descending Christology. In truth, a Christology from below does not have a natural ability to ascend to an adequate recognition of the divinity of Christ any more than the Flatlander can understand the sphere without his "supernatural" elevation. To start from below is to remain stuck below the horizon of transcendence, perhaps having a sense that something new is afoot, yet without the ability to articulate what it is. The created realities that are presupposed by the missions nevertheless retain their integrity. But they exist because there is a mission; indeed, they are consequent upon it. And so even a descending Christology must pay attention to the human condition assumed by the incarnate Son. But it will always recognize within these created effects that which makes them what they are: an outreach of the divine persons, generating *theandric* life.

This applies to the visible as well as the invisible missions. The human nature of Christ, which is the created effect of the Son's visible mission, does not subsist of itself, but is actuated by its assumption into union with the Son. Hence, it is never just humanity. That was the fatal mistake of Nestorius—another theologian who couldn't see the forest because of the trees. This flesh is precisely the Son of God, extending his life to encompass it, and thus to draw all flesh to himself. Conversely, in the invisible mission of the Holy Spirit, the supernatural love infused into our hearts is not simply a created reality but precisely the form of the Spirit's presence. While it has all the natural qualities of love, it is but the *convex* shape of the *concave* Spirit, his imprint upon us. Thus, the liberal reduction of religion and metaphysics to morality is ruled out. God, or the Spirit, is not simply the name that we give to this love, or a symbol referring to this ultimate reality. Rather, love *is* because God is, not vice versa. A moralistic and legalistic reduction of religion is rejected in both Christology and in soteriology. A theology from the missions unapologetically puts God first.

In a post-Enlightenment context, however, this generates much suspicion. Isn't theology sacrificing its objectivity, its intellectual integrity, by thrusting the empirical and critical approach into the background? This is a legitimate concern insofar a theology that simply constructs its object in a subjectivist manner is not desirable. But we can safely conclude after several centuries of Enlightenment thinking that critical thinking and science are not themselves immune from subjective assumptions. This does not justify holding these assumptions, but it is a reminder that objectivity is not achieved by posturing. Moreover, when science calcifies into scientism, and critical thinking devolves into naturalism, they themselves comprise dogmatic obstacles in the way of true knowledge, a kind of Flatland myopia.

At this point, post-Enlightenment standards of objectivity often clash with an authentic theology, premised as they are on the experimental method by which a knowing subject manipulates a docile object. Alas, God is anything but docile. In fact, only to the extent that God himself becomes the subject of the act of knowledge, rather than its mere object, is theology possible. And this is precisely what happens in the missions: in the going forth of the incarnate Word, we are brought to participate in the self-knowledge of the Father! A theological epistemology deprived of the conceptuality of divine missions, both visible and invisible, can at best do little more than explain how human language gestures in the direction of a mysterious *beyond*, ultimately incapable of saying anything positive about it. Without this divine in-reach, we are like the Flatlander who may sense a presence, without knowing what he senses. By the two hands of the Son and the Spirit, reaching out visibly and invisibly, we are included in the trinitarian life, and thus in the eternal divine knowledge and love. We are no longer mere subjects but objects in this knowledge. We have called the missions a tasting of God, a foretaste of the eschatological banquet. In the indwelling of the Trinity we are disposed to enjoy God forever in the wedding feast of the Lamb. This is an experiential—as opposed to an experimental—type of knowledge. Granted, such a knowledge may not be translatable into the language of science or critical thought. But that is because they are ultimately limited and will be utterly surpassed in the transcendent presence of God.

GLOSSARY

Apollinarism	A heretical position according to which the human nature assumed by the Son lacks a human soul, the place of which is taken by the Word.
Created/uncreated grace	The contrast refers to the distinction between the created gifts of grace, which are created dispositions or habits infused in the believer, and the uncreated persons of the Trinity, which indwell the Christian. There is a debate about the logical order between them: do the created gifts mediate the presence of the divine persons, or are they effects of this presence?
Dyothelitism	The doctrine that Christ possesses two natural wills and, correspondingly, two natural operations: divine and human. His divine will is identical with the one will of the Trinity; his human will is the natural will of his human nature, and it can be discerned in the natural desires of Christ: hunger, anguish in the face of death, etc.
Divine operation	The bringing about of particular effects in the world, either through providence (which operates through secondary created causes), or through an intervention in the created cause-effect continuum (special divine action, miracles).

GLOSSARY

Energies (uncreated)	A technical term of Eastern Orthodox theology, influential since the work of Gregory Palamas in the fourteenth century, designating the eternal and natural activity of God. Like the rays of the sun, the uncreated energies surround the essence of God. They are distinguished from the essence, but united to it. In Eastern Orthodox theology, deification takes place through a participation in these energies, since the divine essence cannot be participated in.
Enhypostatic	Refers to the fact that the human nature of Christ does not subsist in a human person, but exclusively in (*en-*) the hypostasis of the Son. Whereas we exist as a combination of human natures and human personal subsistences, Christ is a human nature that exists because it is assumed and personalized by the eternal Son.
Hypostatic union	The union between the person (hypostasis) of the Son and human nature, which is also the visible mission of the Son. The union is hypostatic, which is to say it takes place at the level of the hypostasis, not nature. Thus, Christ is not just divine or just human, but the divine-human person of the Son.
Immanent/economic Trinity	The "immanent" Trinity refers to the relations that exist between the divine persons in eternity, apart from their involvement in creation. These relations would have obtained had there been no creation at all. "Economic" trinity refers to these relationships as they act in the world (creation, redemption, incarnation, etc.). For example, in the immanent Trinity the Son is equal to the Father; in the economic Trinity Christ confesses that "the Father is greater than I" (John 14:28).

GLOSSARY

Inseparable operations	The ancient and universal Christian doctrine that, as the Trinity is one God, so the triune persons always act inseparably as one God, and not simply cooperatively, or collectively, in the world.
Mission	A union between a divine person and a creature, whereby the divine person is present in the world in a new and special way, different from both omnipresence and special divine action.
Mythology	A complex and multilayered term used in this volume to indicate a confusion between the finite effects and movements that take place in this world and their transcendent cause. In mythology, the divine is collapsed into the world and treated as yet another (extraordinary) item in the world. Mythology loses sight of the divine transcendence.
Personal properties (of Son and Spirit)	According to Scripture, the Son is the eternal Word of God, the self-knowledge of the Father (John 1:1; Heb 1:1–2). For that reason, revelation and incarnation are fitting with his personal character. Likewise, the personal property of the Spirit is said to be love (Rom 5:5).
Procession	A generic term used in this volume for the two relations of dependence that obtain between Father-Son and Father-Holy Spirit, whereby the Son is generated by the Father, and the Spirit is spirated by the Father (and the Son, *filioque*).

GLOSSARY

Quasi-formal cause	A manner of expressing the causal relationship between the Son and the human nature of Christ. In an Aristotelian sense, formal causes indicate the nature of a thing. However, formal causes depend on the matter which they "inform," but God does not become the formal cause of anything. Hence, the modified "quasi" indicates that the term should not be taken literally.
Sanctifying grace	That aspect of the grace of God that elevates a creature to a new dimension of existence. Protestants typically view grace as a divine forensic declaration, inaugurating a new covenant, a new relationship between the believer and God. Catholics understand it as *infusing* the believer with supernatural qualities, disposing the believer for union with God.
Simplicity	The doctrine that affirms the absolute aseity (*a se*—from himself), unity, and transcendence of God by denying that any composition exists in him. God is not composed of parts, he has no body, and he has no passions (impassibility). God is not a combination of nature and attributes, for his attributes are his own being and have no independent existence. By contrast, human beings are composed of body and reason. Both attributes have an existence independent of the human beings. In God, his attributes have no existence prior to, or alongside of God, which would destroy his aseity. Thus it is said that God is identical with his attributes: e.g., God is not simply loving, but he is Love itself.

Subsistent relation	A Thomistic way of expressing the nature of the divine persons as relations that subsist. Typically, relations are accidents of substances. In this account of the Trinity, however, relations are not secondary to the substances, but they are at the basis of the substance.

BIBLIOGRAPHY

Aagaard, Anna Marie. "Missio Dei in katolischer Sicht." *Evangelische Theologie* 34 (1974) 420–33.
Abbott, Edwin A. *Flatland: A Romance of Many Dimensions*. New York: Dover, 1992.
Allison, Gregg R., and Andreas J. Köstenberger. *The Holy Spirit*. Nashville: B&H Academic, 2020.
Ambrose. *De Fide* (*On the Christian Faith*). In *St. Ambrose: Select Works and Letters*, edited by Philip Schaff and Henry Wace, translated by H. D. Romestin, 199–314. Nicene and Post-Nicene Fathers, 2nd ser., 10. 1895. Reprint, Peabody, MA: Hendrickson, 1995.
Aquinas, Thomas. *On Love and Charity: Readings from the Commentary on the Sentences of Peter Lombard*. Translated by Peter A. Kwasniewski et al. Washington, DC: Catholic University of America Press, 2012.
———. *Summa contra gentiles: Book 3: Providence: Part I*. Notre Dame: University of Notre Dame Press, 1975.
———. *Summa Theologica*. 5 vols. Translated by the Fathers of the English Dominican Province. Westminster, MD: Christian Classics, 1920.
Augustine. *The Trinity*. Edited by John E. Rotelle. Translated by Edmund Hill. New York: New City, 2015.
Balthasar, Hans Urs von. *Mysterium Paschale: The Mystery of Easter*. San Francisco: Ignatius, 2000.
Bonaventure. *The Breviloquium*. Vol. 2 of *The Works of Bonaventure*. Translated by Jose de Vinck. Paterson, NJ: St. Anthony Guild, 1963.
Bosch, David. *Transforming Mission: Paradigm Shifts in Theology of Mission*. Maryknoll, NY: Orbis, 2011.
Cabasilas, Nicholas. *The Life in Christ*. Translated by Carmino J. deCatanzaro. Crestwood, NY: St. Vladimir's Seminary Press, 1998.
Cantalamessa, Raniero. *Contemplating the Trinity: The Path to Abundant Christian Life*. Translated by Marsha Daigle-Williamson. Ijamsville, MD: Word among Us, 2007.
Coffey, David. "The 'Incarnation' of the Holy Spirit in Christ." *Theological Studies* 45 (1984) 466–80.
Crisp, Oliver. "Did Christ Have a *Fallen* Human Nature?" *International Journal of Systematic Theology* 6.3 (2004) 270–88.
Crowe, Frederick E. "Son of God, Holy Spirit, and World Religions." In *Appropriating the Lonergan Idea*, edited by Michael Vertin, 324–43. Toronto: University of Toronto Press, 2006.

BIBLIOGRAPHY

Denys. *Pseudo-Dionysius: The Complete Works.* Translated by Colm Luibheid. New York: Paulist, 1987.

Dondaine, H. F. "Bulletin de Théologie: La Trinité." *Revue des Sciences Philosophiques et Théologiques* 31 (1947) 433–42.

Edwards, Jonathan. "Excerpt from *The Portion of the Righteous*." In *Jonathan Edwards: Spiritual Writings*, edited by Kyle C. Strobel et al., 163–79. New York: Paulist, 2018.

Emerson, Matthew Y. *"He Descended to the Dead": An Evangelical Theology of Holy Saturday.* Downers Grove, IL: InterVarsity, 2019.

Emery, Gilles. *The Trinitarian Theology of Saint Thomas Aquinas.* Translated by Francesca A. Murphy. Oxford, UK: Oxford University Press, 2007.

Fatehi, Mehrdad. *The Spirit's Relation to the Risen Lord in Paul: An Examination of Its Christological Implications.* Tübingen: Mohr Siebeck, 2000.

Francis, Pope. "A Document on Human Fraternity for World Peace and Living Together." Vatican, Feb. 3–5, 2019. http://www.vatican.va/content/francesco/en/travels/2019/outside/documents/papa-francesco_20190204_documento-fratellanza-umana.html.

Gaine, Simon F. "The Beatific Vision and the Heavenly Mediation of Christ." *Theologica* 2.2 (2018) 123–24.

Gorringe, Timothy. *God's Just Vengeance: Crime, Violence, and the Rhetoric of Salvation.* Cambridge, UK: Cambridge University Press, 1996.

Hill, Edmund. *The Mystery of the Trinity.* New York: HarperCollins, 1986.

Hill, William. "Uncreated Grace—A Critique of Karl Rahner." *Thomist* 27.1 (1963) 333–56.

John Paul II, Pope. "Message of the Holy Father John Paul II to the Youth of the World on the Occasion of the XIX World Youth Day 2004." Vatican, Feb. 22, 2004. http://www.vatican.va/content/john-paul-ii/en/messages/youth/documents/hf_jp-ii_mes_20040301_xix-world-youth-day.html.

Kierkegaard, Søren. *Training in Christianity.* Translated by Walter Lowrie. London: Oxford University Press, 1941.

Legge, Dominic. *The Trinitarian Christology of Thomas Aquinas.* New York: Oxford University Press, 2017.

Leo the Great. "Letter XXVIII." In *Leo the Great, Gregory the Great*, edited by Philip Schaff and Henry Wace, translated by H. D. Romestin, 38–43. Nicene and Post-Nicene Fathers, 2nd ser., 12. 1895. Reprint, New York: Cosimo Classics, 2007.

Lewis, C. S. *Mere Christianity.* 1952. New York: HarperCollins, 2001.

Lombard, Peter. *The Sentences: Book 1: The Mystery of the Trinity.* Translated by Giulio Silano. Toronto: Pontifical Institute of Medieval Studies, 2007.

———. *The Sentences: Book 2: On Creation.* Translated by Giulio Silano. Toronto: Pontifical Institute of Medieval Studies, 2008.

Lonergan, Bernard. *The Triune God: Systematics.* Vol. 12 of *Collected Works of Bernard Lonergan.* Edited by Robert M. Doran and H. Daniel Monsour. Translated by Michael E. Shields. Toronto: University of Toronto Press, 2007.

Lossky, Vladimir. *The Mystical Theology of the Eastern Church.* Crestwood, NY: St. Vladimir's Seminary Press, 1976.

———. "Le problème de la 'vision face à face' et la tradition patristique de Byzance." *Studia Patristica* 2 (1957) 512–37.

———. *The Vision of God.* Translated by Asheleigh Moorhouse. London: Faith, 1963.

Maloney, George. *Inward Stillness.* Denville, NJ: Dimension, 1976.

BIBLIOGRAPHY

Maximus. "Opusculum 7." In *Maximus the Confessor*, 170–90. London: Routledge, 1996.

McCormack, Bruce. "The Ontological Presuppositions of Barth's Doctrine of the Atonement." In *The Glory of the Atonement: Biblical, Historical, and Practical Perspectives*, edited by Frank A. James III and Charles Hill, 346–66. Downers Grove, IL: InterVarsity, 2004.

Moltmann, Jürgen. *The Church in the Power of the Spirit: A Contribution to Messianic Ecclesiology.* London, SCM, 1977.

———. *The Crucified God.* Translated by R. A. Wilson and John Bowden. London: SCM, 1974.

———. *The Trinity and the Kingdom of God*, Translated by Margaret Kohl. London: SCM, 1981.

Owen, John. *The Glory of Christ*. Vol. 1 of *The Works of John Owen*. Edited by William H. Gould. Edinburgh: Banner of Truth, 1965.

Phan, Peter. *Being Religious Interreligiously: Asian Perspectives on Interfaith Dialogue*. Maryknoll, NY: Orbis, 2004.

Pitstick, Lyra. *Light in Darkness: Hans Urs von Balthasar and the Catholic Doctrine of Christ's Descent into Hell*. Grand Rapids: Eerdmans, 2007.

Pohle, Joseph. *The Divine Trinity: A Dogmatic Treatise*. St. Louis: Herder, 1915.

Rahner, Karl. "Jesus Christ in the Non-Christian Religions." In *Theological Investigations: Jesus, Man and the Church*, translated by Margaret Kohl, 17:39–50. London: Darton, Longman & Todd, 1981.

———. "Some Implications of the Scholastic Concept of Uncreated Grace." In *Theological Investigations*, translated by Cornelius Ernst, 1:319–46. Baltimore, MD: Helicon, 1961.

Rosin, H. H. *Missio Dei: An Examination of the Origin, Contents and Function of the Term in Protestant Missiological Discussion*. Leiden: Inter-University Institute for Missiological and Ecumenical Research, 1972.

Ruusbroec, John. *The Spiritual Espousals and Other Works*. New York: Paulist, 1985.

Schillebeeckx, Edward. "Ascension and Pentecost." *Worship* 35.6 (1961) 336–63.

Smeaton, George. *The Doctrine of the Holy Spirit*. Edinburgh: T&T Clark, 1882.

Stăniloae, Dumitru. "The Procession of the Holy Spirit from the Father and His Relation to the Son, as the Basis of Our Deification and Adoption." In *Spirit of God, Spirit of Christ: Ecumenical Reflections on the* Filioque *Controversy*, edited by Lukas Vischer, 174–86. London: World Council of Churches, 1981.

Stump, Eleonore. *Atonement*. Oxford Studies in Analytical Theology. Oxford, UK: Oxford University Press, 2019.

———. "Dante's Hell, Aquinas's Moral Theory, and the Love of God." *Canadian Journal of Philosophy* 16.2 (1986) 181–98.

Tanner, Kathryn. *Christ the Key*. Cambridge, UK: Cambridge University Press, 2010.

Torrell, Jean Pierre. *Spiritual Master*. Vol. 2 of *Saint Thomas Aquinas*. Translated by Robert Royal. Washington, DC: Catholic University Press, 1996.

Vidu, Adonis. *Atonement, Law, and Justice: The Cross in Historical and Cultural Contexts*. Grand Rapids: Baker Academic, 2014.

———. *The Same God Who Works All Things: Inseparable Operations in Trinitarian Theology*. Grand Rapids: Eerdmans, 2021.

———. "Triune Agency, East and West: Uncreated Energies or Created Effects?" *Perichoresis* 18.1 (2020) 57–75.

Witsius, Herman. *Sacred Dissertations on the Apostles' Creed.* 2 vols. Translated by Donald Fraser. Glasgow: Khull, Blackie & Co, 1823.
World Council of Churches. *The Church for Others and the Church for the World: A Quest for Structures for Missionary Congregations. Final Report of the Western European Working Group and North American Working Group of the Department of Studies in Evangelism.* Geneva: World Council of Churches, 1967.
Yong, Amos. *Beyond the Impasse: Toward a Pneumatological Theology of Religions.* Eugene, OR: Wipf & Stock, 2014.
Zizioulas, John D. *Being as Communion: Studies in Personhood and the Church.* Crestwood, NY: St. Vladimir's Seminary Press, 1993.

Printed in Great Britain
by Amazon